"I first became aware of Josh Shipp when I was hosting TRL on MTV. He came on the show and gave teens solid advice that was funny and easily understood. Josh's book does the same thing. It urges you to get off your butt and take some action for improving your life—regardless of your age. Life is short. So, what are you waiting for? Read this book!"

—DAMIEN FAHEY, MTV

"Josh Shipp totally gets it. His approach to getting teens to relate, open up, and get inspired is truly wonderful. So many authors have no idea how to really connect to teens and tweens. Let your kids learn to take over the world and feel awesome doing it!"

—VANESSA VAN PETTEN, YOUTHOLOGIST
AND CREATOR OF RADICALPARENTING.COM

"I LOVE THIS BOOK. He is spot-on in the advice he shares to help teens create not only a fulfilling, connected life but a life that they can TRULY dominate! I am certain that if teens read this book they will avoid the perpetually annoying quarter-life crisis that comes in their twenties because they will have gotten the secret message of it all: Life is short. So hurry up and begin living the one you want."

—JESS WEINER, AUTHOR, SELF-ESTEEM EXPERT

"'Be the hero of your own story' gets a twenty-first-century makeover with edgy candor, frank advice, and raw, real truisms you just can't duck-n-dodge. Simply put: If you don't choose to control your own world, then people will call the shots for you. The drama will control you—other people's expectations will control you. The villains (your past, your fears, bad relationships, addictions) will ALL line up to control you. . . . Playful, poignant, and spot-on in its Yoda-like wisdom, Josh's new book lands a loud and clear message: Teens, if you don't dominate your own world, someone else will."

—AMY JUSSEL, FOUNDER/EXECUTIVE DIRECTOR OF SHAPING YOUTH

"One triumph of a book. It is hard to get a chance at an early age to do anything other than what we are told to do, and with Shipp's book, teens have a stellar shot of accomplishing their dreams, while other teens are eating peanut butter and jelly sandwiches and chilling on seesaws."

—SKYLER STONE, COMEDY CENTRAL

"I love this book and I love Josh Shipp for writing it. Yeah, he's in your face but, like he says, he's always on your side. With The Teen's Guide to World Domination you'll get what you need to dominate the only part of any world you've got a shot at. That would be your own world, as in your thoughts, feelings, and choices. So quit stressing yourself out trying to get other people to do and be what you want. Instead, pick up Josh's guide. Learning to get the life you want starts here."

—ANNIE FOX, AUTHOR OF *TOO STRESSED TO THINK?*
AND *MIDDLE SCHOOL CONFIDENTIAL*

"Josh Shipp will knock you on your butt with his life experience and give you the best advice he never got. He'll also make you laugh for the whole crazy ride."

—MELISSA WALKER, AUTHOR, FOUNDER OF IHEARTDAILY

"Best. Book. Ever. Josh Shipp is pee-your-pants hilarious and blow-your-mind profound in this entertaining and inspiring book that just might save your life. It's fresh. It's brilliant. It's everything you want to be. You have to have it."

—MICHAEL BUCKLEY, YOUTUBE SENSATION, *WHAT THE BUCK*

THE TEEN'S GUIDE TO WORLD DOMINATION. Copyright © 2010 by
Hey Josh, LLC. All rights reserved. Printed in the United States
of America. For information, address St. Martin's Press,
175 Fifth Avenue, New York, N.Y. 10010.

www.stmartins.com

BOOK DESIGN BY AMANDA DEWEY

Written with help from Michael Colletto, Jordan Green,
and Dot&Cross.

Edited by Michael Colletto and Molly Young.

Library of Congress Cataloging-in-Publication Data

Shipp, Josh.
    The teen's guide to world domination : advice on life, liberty, and the
pursuit of awesomeness / Josh Shipp.—1st ed.
            p. cm.
    ISBN 978-0-312-64154-2
    1. Teenagers—Life skills guides.   2. Teenagers—Conduct of life.
3. Interpersonal relations in adolescence.   I. Title.
    HQ796.S4499 2010
    646.700835—dc22   2010022069

First Edition: August 2010

10 9 8 7 6 5 4 3 2 1

The **Teen's** Guide

W⭐RLD
DOMINATION

Advice on Life, Liberty,

and the Pursuit of

Awesomeness

josh shipp

St. Martin's Griffin ❧ New York

TO MY AMAZING FOSTER PARENTS,

RODNEY & CHRISTINE WEIDENMAIER.

THIS IS ALL YOUR FAULT.

Contents

Part 3:
How to Dominate Your World   115

Part 4:
How to Dominate Today, Tomorrow, and Forever 263

THIS IS REQUIRED READING

// If you skip this introduction, I will find you and slap you. I'm not joking.

Good evening, teenage human.

Pleasure to meet you. I'm Josh Shipp, aka the guy on the cover of this book whose hair looks like a Chia Pet. Aka the guy who just threatened to slap you. And meant it.

I don't always threaten to slap people. I only do that when it's important, you know? Slapping people usually gets their attention. And I need your attention right now because your life is at stake.

"Excuse me, Josh?" Yes, you heard me. Your life is at stake.

No, you're not dying, so don't panic and call 911. This is good news, so lean in and listen closely.

You get to choose how you live your life.

You can either dominate it . . . or do nothing, and let other people call the shots. You can either do exactly what you want to do or let other people tell you what to do.

And it doesn't matter who you are or what you've got going for you (or against you). For all I know, you could've just stolen this book. You could be robbing me right now. Well, I'm kind of OK with that. I'm delighted you stole/bought/received/inherited from your deceased relative/illegally downloaded/in some other way acquired this book. Why? Because I want you to read it. Plus, my face is on the cover, and I just think that's awesome slash awkward.

Before we begin, you've gotta understand something:

// I didn't write this book because I'm perfect.

I don't have all the answers. Sure, I'm a young dude who spends his days giving advice to teens—in high school auditoriums, on TV (you may have seen me on MTV, CNN, NBC, FOX, or Comedy Central), on the radio, on people's front yards (without their permission), and online at HeyJosh.com. Recently, I was named to *Inc. Magazine*'s "30 Under 30" list of "America's Coolest Young Entrepreneurs." (Very flattering.) I was seventeen when I decided this is what I wanted to do with my life and, since then, I've built a really successful career. People from literally all around the world now consider me a leading authority on teen communication. Crazy, right? I get 100,000 e-mails from teens every year asking for my advice, and I've spoken to well over a million teens . . . and counting. It's kind of funny, really—I used to get kicked out for talking in class, and now I get paid for it!

But I don't give advice because I know it all. Or because I'm supersmart and have thirty-seven PhD's. Far from it.

I give advice for a living because I'm horrible at manual labor. Kind of uncoordinated. Really bad with directions. And a little bit lazy. I'm just a guy who's made a lot of mistakes, gone through a lot of painful experiences, and learned some valuable lessons along the way.

I was left at the hospital by my birth parents, so I know what it's like to be abandoned. To this day I've never met my parents or anyone related to me. I grew up in several different foster homes. I've been kicked out, abused, forgotten about, and written off by others. I've been overweight, picked on, and suicidal, and I've felt like my life had zero point. I even spent a little time in jail. Not exactly the biography of a guy who's got it all together.

I don't tell you all this to depress you. Or to make you feel sorry for me. Trust me, that is not my style.

I tell you this to communicate that, whatever you're going through—whatever you're dealing with—whether your life is perfect or perfectly horrible, you have what it takes to dominate your world. And I wrote this book to show you how it's done. 'Cause if I can do it, you can.

I don't think I'm better than you. Smarter than you. Or have it all figured out.

Just 'cause I'm an author or a motivational speaker or an "expert" or whatever doesn't mean my life is perfect. I have bad days. I yell at my friends. I don't always try my best. I get upset. Pissed off. Show up late. Sometimes I don't bathe regularly.

But I'm always trying to get better. I don't know about you, but

I want my life to matter. I don't want to get dragged down or pushed around. I want to do what I'm good at—what I love to do—and get paid for it. I want to be happy, and I want to make a difference. I want to surround myself with people who see the best in me. I wanna be a guy my friends can count on. That's the kind of life I want to live. And I want to help you to do the same.

Disclaimer Number One

I'm a smart aleck, and I'm random, so you better be packing heat. And by heat I mean Google. I'm not afraid to tackle a serious topic and then throw an obscure YouTube reference into the mix. We don't have to be all serious and stuck-up to discuss serious topics.

Disclaimer Number Two

I am not your dad. Or your teacher. Or your parole officer. Think of me as your older brother. I don't think I know it all, but I think I've got some pretty solid ideas. My style is in your face, but on your side. We can laugh and joke around and have a good time. But if you whine or complain or pull some crap as to why you can't accomplish something . . . I'll call you out on it. Got it?

Disclaimer Number Three

Read this book however you want. Cover to cover if you're an overachiever or, you know, a normal literate human. If you're like me and have the attention span of a small can of Mr. Pibb (huh?), feel free to skip to whatever chapter strikes your fancy. Use it as a kick in the pants and then apply it to your life. Word of warning:

If you skip Sections 1 and 2, you're going to be very, very confused when I start calling your teacher a robot and your girlfriend a puppy (unless you're actually dating a puppy, in which case, I can't help you), so proceed at your own intellectual peril.

In your face, but on your side,

// josh shipp

P.S. Up Up Down Down Left Right Left Right B A select start— just because I use cheats doesn't mean I'm not smart.

P.P.S. Stop playing FarmVille right now. It's a lame use of your time, doesn't make you better looking, and produces no real vegetation.

Part 1

FUNDAMENTALS of WORLD DOMINATION

1.

Total World Domination = Epic Fail

// Let's face it: Total world domination never works.

(OK, you're probably confused. Maybe you're wondering if you're actually reading the right book. You probably read the title and picked it up thinking world domination sounded like a pretty good idea, but then you opened it up and—what the . . . ?—the title of the first part seems to contradict the title of the book! Yes, I am tricksy. What were you expecting? This ain't no textbook. We need to understand each other before we go any further: I operate in one way and one way only—always in your face, but on your side. Copy? OK, so, let's clear the air. You are asking, "Josh, are you actually contradicting the title of your book in the first paragraph?" Yes, I am. Onward . . .)

When I was just a little boy wonder, there was this cartoon

called *Animaniacs*. You probably don't remember it, but the show featured a recurring segment called "Pinky and the Brain" about two genetically enhanced lab mice: Pinky, an idiot, and Brain, a diabolical genius much like yourself. Every episode began with these two lines of dialogue:

> **Pinky:** *Gee, Brain, what are we going to do tonight?*
> **Brain:** *The same thing we do every night, Pinky: Try to take over the world!*

And try they did. Using all manner of cunning schemes and high-tech absurdities, Brain—with often disastrous "help" from Pinky—would mastermind a plan for total world domination.

It wasn't just "Pinky and the Brain." Every show I grew up on, from *Care Bears* (did I just admit to watching *Care Bears*?) to *Masters of the Universe* (much more manly) to *Transformers,* had a villain trying to subjugate the other characters. (Confession: I don't even know what "subjugate" means, but my book editor told me not to talk down to teens and to challenge them with big words. Well, I have challenged myself and failed. I am crying right now.) These villains went by names like Professor Coldheart, Skeletor, Megatron, and Monty Burns. They often emitted evil, cackling laughs. They nearly all had henchmen, and sometimes they had mustaches . . . which stirred up jealousy in me due to my complete inability to grow facial hair, even to this day. Tear.

Fast-forward to today: Dark wizard Lord Voldemort and his Death Eaters terrorize humanity in the Harry Potter series; the merciless Volturi cause trouble for Bella in the Twilight saga; and, after all these years, Decepticon overlord Megatron is still bent on destroying Earth and everyone on it. All of these villains—and every villain from our books to the big screen—are after the same thing: Absolute power, complete control, and total world domination.

But power-hungry villains aren't just the stuff of fiction. In fact, the villain's quest for world domination is a classic case of art imitating life. When I was in school, the only homework my foster parents could ever force my ADD brain to focus on was history, particularly the stories about real-world dudes who built vast empires—like the Egyptian pharaohs, Xerxes I, and countless other emperors, kings, queens, warlords, generals, and dictators. Let me tell you, actual history is really just a big soap opera of crazy people trying to take over the world. But here's what I discovered. These historical figures—from Hitler to Napoléon to Genghis Khan to Alexander the Great—all had one thing in common:

(Actually, they had a lot in common—egos the size of Texas, an insatiable thirst for power and wealth, a common serial killer's disregard for human life—but I'm talking about *besides* that.)

None of them ever succeeded. That's right, not one.

Sure, they had people running scared for a while, and some of these guys conquered huge chunks of territory. But no matter how big their army, how prosperous their economy, how abundant their resources, how advanced their technology, how brilliant their devious plan, or how epically bushy their facial hair (I'm looking at you, Genghis) . . . *they could never quite pull it off.* Their empires always crumbled.

To this day, no one has been able to take over the entire

world—not in cartoons, not in books, not in movies, and definitely not in history!

// Yet the villains keep trying

Despite the dismal track record of ambitious tyrants who've tried and died before them, modern-day villains remain fascinated by and fixated on their personal quests for world domination. Ancient rulers tried to conquer the world in search of mythical items like the fountain of youth, gold (btw, what's with all those gold-bar infomercials on TV after 2 A.M.?), or ultimate glory. But these days, it's usually about political power, natural resources, weapons, and cold hard cash. It seems that everyone is looking for that magical force or item that will allow them to control everyone else or give them a leg up in the race of world domination.

Fortunately, the vast majority of these selfish and destructive individuals won't become rulers of nations or commanders of armies. But, something you need to understand is that it doesn't take an army, a giant moon-laser, or a mustache to try to control others' lives.

Would-be villains are still out to dominate other people's worlds every day, and I'm not just talking about national security or terrorist threats. Lean in for this one:

Your world is under attack by an assortment of villains right here and right now.

I'm serious! Through manipulation and physical strength or through passive-aggressiveness and psychological warfare, there are villains in your life today trying to control your world for their own gain.

Let me be clear to make sure you heard me. The villains are real and they are coming for you. But if you don't believe me, this book isn't going to make any sense to you and you're not going to last.

In fact, there may be villains among us right now, even reading this book. Are you a villain? Are you? Huh? Don't look away from the page—I'm not kidding, here. Think about it, you DID pick up a book called *The Teen's Guide to World Domination*! YOU might actually be a villain trying to control others' lives for your own gain. But let's be honest, I don't entirely blame you: World domination does have a certain appeal, doesn't it? Even to noble citizens like us.

Sure, people like you and me probably don't really aspire to overthrow governments or create secret lairs guarded by sharks with lasers on their heads in order to bring small nations to their knees while our merciless conquest is broadcast live on CNN with Larry King (the emperor of suspenders). In my experience, most people don't want to do that. Most people aren't psychotic megalomaniacs. (Ooh . . . "megalomaniac"! How's *that* for challenging teens? I think it means either a crazy person or something about breeding giant LEGO blocks; I heard it on a random AM radio station and it seemed to work here.)

The idea of getting other people to do what we want . . . well, that sounds kinda fancy, doesn't it? But trust me, controlling other people isn't fancy. It's awful, and you and I both know your grandmother would be ashamed of you if she knew you were doing this.

Beneath the surface, grandiose (how do you like them apples, editor?) plans to dominate the world are usually about something far less impressive. Often, it's because we want something and we're not willing to play nice to get it. We don't feel good about who we are, so, to get what we want, we have to knock someone else down. We don't feel powerful, so we find someone weaker to control. That's what happened with Napoléon and Hitler. And take a look at Kim Jong Il from North Korea! That dude is 5'3"; talk about a complex! He just got extremely good at controlling people and started wearing platform shoes to appear more manly. (I must say that I understand his pain, being just 5'8" myself; I often refer to myself as a "man-boy.") But whether you are short or tall, taking advantage of those weaker than you is just plain wrong.

Bottom line: The traditional quest for total world domination NEVER succeeds, it USUALLY stems from ugly motives, and ALWAYS, without a doubt, hurts other people.

It's time to recognize that the quest for total world domination isn't all it's cracked up to be. It's time to choose a new battle, set a new goal. Instead of trying to conquer a small country or even just conquering your own high school classroom, let's leave everyone else alone for a while and focus on something else, something that is actually doable!

Here's the thing: There's a bigger, more important challenge out there and we've all overlooked it. Any coward can try to control someone else's life, but it takes a hero to face the biggest challenge of them all: Dominating your own world.

Turns out that all the villainous people throughout history aren't just evil or crazy; ultimately, they were all cowards. They didn't have the guts to take on the challenge of dominating their own world, so instead they focused on playing dirty so they could control others. But controlling others is nothing compared to the challenge of dominating your own life.

In fact, most people can't do it. They fold. They give up. They say they're interested, but at the first sign of struggle, they bail. Why? Because anything worth doing is always going to be hard. Think about anything in your life that has been epic. Was it easy? NO, but was it worth it? Of course! And this will be, too. Trust me.

So, here's my question: Are you willing to dominate your own world?

If you can't answer "yes," just shut the book, eBay it, and use the money to buy yourself an assortment of suckers because that's what you are, a sucker, and that's the way you're choosing to live your life. I hope you like the flavor.

If, however, you are one of the few, one of the heroes—if you're a true revolutionary, someone with an underground resistance mentality—then now is the time. Now is the time to stop trying to dominate the whole world and start trying to dominate your own.

That's where we're headed. That's what this book is all about.

So, who's with me? If you're not with me, take another lick of your sucker and shut the book. But if you're in, turn the page.

Game on.

2.

Dominate Your World... or Someone Else Will

// Redefining world domination

So . . . you in? You think you've got what it takes? Alright. Let's do this.

First, it's time for a radical redefinition of "world domination." Since no one has ever been able to dominate the world—and those who still try are usually motivated by ugly, selfish characteristics like insecurity and greed—I've come up with a better plan. Instead of wasting time and soiling your soul trying to dominate the whole world and control other people, set your sights on a more personal conquest:

Dominate your own world!

Yup, that's it. It's simple—you can't control what your

brother, mother, or lady friend does, so stop trying! At the end of the day, there is only one person that you can control . . . YOU.

Ready for the secret to get exactly what you want out of your life? This secret won't cost you three easy payments of $19.99, it won't come with a money-back guarantee, and it won't slap your troubles away with the slap-slap-slapchop.

// Here's the secret to dominating your world

There isn't one.

"Wow, Josh," you may be thinking, "this book sucks. You title the book *The Teen's Guide to World Domination,* but then tell me world domination never works. Next you sell me on the idea you can make my life better, and now you're telling me that there is no secret? While you're at it, would you like to kick my dog in the face?"

Listen, calm down. I'm not trying to depress you, but I am being real with you. I wish I could give you the magic formula, but I can't. It doesn't exist. And if someone else tries to tell you different, they're lying to you.

There is only one way to dominate your world: You have to choose to do it. *Choose to dominate your world.*

You want to be successful in life? You want to be awesome? You want to live with confidence and purpose, and be one of those people everyone looks up to and respects? If you want your life to matter, to make a difference, and if you want to be able to look back on your life, when you're old and fading, and say, "That was epic . . . I wouldn't change a thing," then listen up.

Choosing to control your world is a minute-by-minute, day-by-day decision you have to make. This isn't a onetime decision. It is a conversation-by-conversation, moment-by-moment way of life. If you don't choose to control your world, other people will call the shots for you. The drama will control you. Other people's expectations will control you. The villains, your past, your fears, bad relationships, and addictions will all line up to control you.

If you don't take responsibility—and take action—you've already lost, and no secret magical formula will make things better. That's just reality for ya.

So, this is the new definition of world domination:

It's not about dominating THE world;
it's about choosing to dominate YOUR world.

And dominating your world doesn't mean you've got to be better than everyone else. It doesn't mean you have to be a jerk and step on people to get to the top. You simply have to choose to be YOUR best.

If you are willing to choose to dominate your world and if you are willing to listen, I can show you how to be awesome. No secrets needed.

// Maybe I'm getting ahead of myself here . . .

There's a catch to being awesome: Being awesome is never convenient.

Choosing to dominate your world takes hard work.

Maybe you think you've got more important things to think about: That never-ending geyser of homework, after-school practice, those crucial text messages piling up on your phone. Maybe you're not that interested in being awesome and dominating your world. Maybe you're perfectly content living an average, boring, ultimately lame life.

Or maybe you're just trying to survive. You're too stressed out. You're too busy. You're in a funk. Maybe you're barely keeping your head above water and you're miles from shore in shark-infested waters (metaphorically speaking).

Or maybe you're just scared. Or lazy.

Don't be. Look, I warned you: Being awesome and dominating your world will never, ever, in any dimension of reality, be easy. Now don't start weeping—I said this would be challenging, not impossible. You can do this. Literally anyone can do this if they're willing to try, and try hard.

Think about the following success stories:

Rock bands start in garages.
Geniuses spend lonely hours in libraries and laboratories.
World-class athletes stay late to practice.

Entrepreneurs pour their lives into ideas that everyone else thinks
   are stupid.
World changers challenge the system and are often hated for it.
Loving mothers are rarely thanked.

The people you admire most—the people you really aspire to
be like—each one of them makes a decision every day.

What's the difference between you and them? They choose,
each day, to be that awesome person, whatever it takes.

Will you choose that?

// If you don't dominate your world, someone else will

Here's the thing: Your story won't write itself. It's either going to
be an autobiography or a biography. You write it yourself or you
let someone else do it. If you want to settle for the passenger seat
and go along for the ride, that's fine; just realize this means that
someone else is driving, and you can't complain about where you
end up.

Let me put it this way:

World domination requires CHOICE, and each day you make
a choice (whether you realize it or not). So you've got two choices:
Dominate your world . . . or don't.

"But wait!" a corner of your brain objects. "There's a third option! Can't I just put this off for a bit? What if I just dominate my
world later? Like, when I'm older."

Hate to break it to ya, but that third option is just a cop-out. Allow me to illustrate: Your best friend's dad surprises her with tickets to go see her favorite band (incidentally, also your favorite band) in concert tomorrow night . . . and she has an extra ticket to invite a friend. Naturally, she asks you. You have two choices: Yes, no, or the third option, "um . . . let me think about it"/"maybe later." You choose "maybe later" . . . and, twenty-four hours later, "maybe" becomes "no" by default—the concert goes on without you, and your friend takes someone else. You missed your chance. And you sit at home and weep 'cause tonight coulda been a good good night.

Here's my point: In life, there's no choice at all if you don't make a decision. Choosing not to choose is a choice just like any other, and a weak choice at that. In the end, you'll just be swept along.

Your opportunities are narrowing all the time, whether you want them to or not. If you don't take ownership of your world, someone else will land your slot in architecture school. Someone else will get the scholarship for creative writing. Someone else will get that perfect job interview. Someone else will marry your dream guy or swoop in on your dream girl. And you will end up wandering through your life without any purpose or direction. Most likely without car insurance.

You'll be average, unremarkable, lost in the crowd—dominated by villains.

Ever seen *The Dog Whisperer*? It's about this guy, Cesar Millan, who can seriously put any dog in its place. People come to him and they're practically being tormented by their pets—these dogs totally dominate their owners. These are the craziest, meanest, yippiest dogs in the world, and Cesar teaches their owners how to control them. It's like magic; I mean, this guy is a master. But his secret is simple: *Be the pack leader.* Dogs live in packs, so they see you as part of their pack. Every pack has a leader, so if you don't step up and assert yourself as the pack leader, your dog becomes the boss by default. And if your dog is the pack leader, he does whatever he wants—he tears up your shoes, bites your neighbor, poops on the carpet, and jumps on you when you're sleeping. You don't have to tell a dog, "You're in control here"—he takes control automatically as soon as you stop being the pack leader. If you don't dominate your world, your dog will take over as the pack leader. And trust me, if you don't dominate your world, having your dog take control of your life will be the LEAST of your worries.

If you don't take responsibility for dominating your world and defending yourself against the onslaught of villains, the villains have already won.

In fact, I know your world is already under attack. You could probably name a couple of people right now who have the ability to tick you off so bad you can't even think straight. Or maybe there is someone in your life who scares the pants off you. Maybe it's a parent, a teacher, your boyfriend, or a coach who is manipulating your world with mysterious powers of mind control. These are your personal villains who still believe that world domination is possible and profitable, and right now, they are dominating you.

Why are you letting them do it? Let me teach you how to choose to take control of your own world. Remember: If you're NOT dominating your own life, someone else is. The sooner you realize this, the sooner you can begin choosing your own path and becoming who you want to be.

Whether you realize it or not, you're telling a story, and you have a choice: Tell an EPIC story or tell a lame one.

Meanwhile, there are people out there—like bullies and bad boyfriends and losers—who are trying to control your story. And there are people—like parents and teachers and counselors—who are trying to tell your story for you. Don't let them.

Choose to dominate your world. Tell an epic story. Make your own decisions . . . or you'll end up being one of those porch grouches hollering at people to get off their lawn, unhappy and bitter at the end of a sad and disappointing life.

Choosing to dominate your world isn't easy. Sure, most people *want* to dominate their worlds, but few are willing to put in the hard work to actually do it. And it does take work.

I can't dominate your world for you. Your mom can't dominate your world for you. Nor can your teachers or your friends or the president.

Only you can.

What your world needs is a hero.

3.

It Takes a Hero

Now, maybe you're thinking I'm crazy. (I never said I wasn't . . .) "Josh," you say with your right hand pointed toward the sky, "my life is comprised of pure glory and my quest proceedeth unobstructed. I see no evidence of a devious dark sorcerer or a mischievous mastermind set on controlling mine fate. No one controls me. I'm the pack leader. I'm my own boss."

Really. Think so? That's cute. You are sounding dangerously indifferent about your life right now. Then stop wasting your time and give this book to a friend. Why? Because 99.9 percent of the people I know, including me, are looking for something better.

OK, good for you, but OH MY GOSH YOUR FACE IS ON FIRE!!!

Sorry, that was a bit dramatic. There's really no need to panic. Please point the fire extinguisher away from your eyes; you could blind yourself. I was just trying to get your attention. If you're feeling all comfortable and cozy in your little life, I have some bad news:

// If you don't feel threatened, you've already been beaten

Here's the thing about villains: They ALWAYS pose a threat. The good guys notice villains and struggle endlessly against them. If your world doesn't feel threatened, there are only three possible explanations:

1. **You're bad.** This means that you are actually a villain, not a hero. Sometimes villains pick fights among themselves ('cause they're belligerent like that), but for the most part, they'll join forces and sit around a giant table and scheme about working together to crush the hero or heroine. So, if you don't feel threatened by any villains, that could be because you're a villain yourself. You don't feel the threat because you ARE the threat. I hate to tell you this, but guess what? If you're a villain, you're a coward. Why don't you quit trying to control other people and get a grip on your own life for once?

2. **You're blind.** Most people don't have any idea how to identify villains. Villains are often sneaky, and sometimes they don't stand out from the crowd. Unlike in the movies, villains won't necessarily wear hooded black robes or have sinister facial hair. In other words, you may not feel the threat because you can't SEE the threat. You just think all the villains walking

around are normal, friendly faces that can be trusted. It's time
to open your eyes.

3.   **You're beaten.** Villains don't waste their time on people who
have already been crushed. So, you might not feel threatened
because you've already been dominated. Villains don't mess
with people who aren't doing anything of value. You're not a
threat to villains if your goal is to live in your parents' basement and eat Cheetos until you're forty.

Now, don't get depressed on me; there's a strangely inspirational
silver lining to this cloud of depression: If you're feeling threatened—if you notice the villains trying to take you down—that's
actually a really good sign. It means you just might be an up-and-
coming hero. High five.

So . . . now what? Now that you know there are villains out to
dominate your world and that your world is under attack right
now, what's a young human to do?

Well, if you take your cues from the world around you, you'll
notice that . . .

// Common folk run

The average person is concerned with one thing: Getting by. They
don't want to rock the boat or stir up trouble or draw too much
attention to themselves. They just want what they want, and they
want to be happy and, generally, left alone. So, when a villain shows
up, what does the average person do?

Run.

Common folk also like to hide. Faint. Mess themselves. Weep like a small child. Maybe—just maybe—they'll work up enough guts to squeak like a gerbil as they roll over, squinch their eyes shut, and wait to die. Let's be honest: The average person is a lot like that guy from the first *Jurassic Park* movie who, at the first sign of trouble, abandons the kids in the Jeep, flees in terror, and hides in the outhouse in a desperate attempt to save himself . . . where he quickly (and predictably) becomes the first casualty of the film—eaten by a *T. rex* right off the ol' crapper. Really pathetic.

And if average people are cornered—if the villains find them in their oh-so-secret hiding spot, whimpering under the table—they'll just surrender. "You want to take over my world? Fine! It's yours! Please don't kill me."

You want to live a quiet, comfortable life? Then just surrender to the villains now. If you don't give them any trouble—if you behave yourself and play by their rules—they'll leave you alone. All you need to do is blend in: Accept what people tell you at face value, live the way others expect you to, never question authority, and jump through hoops.

If that kind of life sounds good to you, don't feel bad; most people choose that life. You won't be alone, you'll fit in just fine, and the villains will let you play in their yard with everyone else who surrendered. You'll be dominated, but you'll be safe, comfortable, and unchallenged. Kind of like that gerbil.

So, if safety and comfort and an easy life is what you really want, well, world domination isn't for you. Go ahead and stop reading, close the book, and get used to other people controlling your life.

But know this:

// Heroes stand and fight

Let's be frank with one another: Life is hard for heroes. They're constantly under attack, they're misunderstand, they're rarely given the credit they're due, and sometimes they are blamed for causing trouble. But the world falls into darkness without them.

The world needs heroes.

YOUR world needs a hero. If you're not a hero, your world doesn't stand a chance.

So, summon your inner hero! Only heroes can see the villains, resist the temptation to become one, and put up a fight.

Heroes are protectors, defenders, role models, and champions. But they are also perfectly ordinary people. What sets them apart from common folk is their *response* to challenges. When their world is under attack and the odds are stacked against them, instead of running away or surrendering like most people, heroes display courage—even a willingness to sacrifice themselves to protect others.

Villains HATE heroes. Heroes don't go down quietly. Heroes don't let villains take over the world. If you want to reclaim your life from the villains and dominate your world, you've gotta learn how to be a hero. If you're a hero, the villains will tremble.

But here's the catch: You don't get to be a hero by squeezing into a spandex costume and calling yourself "Villain Crusher." You've gotta meet certain qualifications . . . and play by the rules.

4.

Heroes Play by the Rules (A How-to Guide)

Other people—villains—are trying to dominate your world, and only a hero can stop them.

So, the question becomes, will you be that hero?

Now, I know some of you don't feel like hero material. But you've gotta realize going into this, you don't become a hero overnight. I mean, sure, you might get bitten by a genetically modified spider and wake up with superhuman powers, but even then it's gonna take time before you figure out how to control your new abilities and handle them responsibly. There's always training involved. Think about it: Harry Potter was just a runty misfit kid with a scar on his forehead living under the stairs before he went to Hogwarts; Batman started off as a bitter rich kid; Luke Skywalker began as a whiny farm boy on a desert world; Iron Man was a self-centered *villain* of a dude; Tai in *Clueless* was a clumsy pot smoker before she became a megababe with a heart of gold; Frodo—I mean, he was just an ordinary *hobbit*, for Pete's sake—you think a three-foot-tall barefooted being bubbling with carefree innocence would just up and decide to take on the Dark Lord of Mordor? I don't think so.

Heroes aren't born; they're made. And it's often a process of self-discovery and self-sacrifice.

Here's what it takes:

// Heroes know who they are

Heroes define themselves and own their own identity. Heroes know their strengths and weaknesses, likes and dislikes, passions and goals.

It's often easier for us to express what we don't like or aren't good at. Fine. Start there. For me, I don't like details. I suck at directions. I get lost in my own neighborhood—it's embarrassing. ("Off route—recalculating.") I'm great in bigger groups, but I'm a little bashful one-on-one. I love being around people, but I shut down if I don't have enough time by myself to recharge.

I used to think the things I wasn't great at were weaknesses or things that needed to change. That if I just "put my head down, worked harder, and tried really hard," they would change. Truth is, they're part of who I am.

My strengths AND my weaknesses make me, me. Just like yours make you uniquely you.

When you embrace all that and stop lying to yourself ("no, no—I swear, I really am outgoing"), you become stronger because you are cool with who you are. To be a hero, you have to be proud of who you are and know you are strong. You won't always *feel* strong—no one does—but you do have gifts and interests other people don't have. If it helps, think of them as your superpowers.

This whole "knowing who you are" thing is harder than it sounds and can be an ongoing process, but don't worry, I'll lend you a hand in Chapter 15; we'll get all this identity stuff squared away so when a villain sneers at you and asks, "And who do you think *you* are?" you can tell them EXACTLY who you are, shut 'em up, and send 'em packing.

// Heroes believe they have what it takes

Dominating your world requires confidence. Confidence comes from knowing who you are. Confidence doesn't mean being arrogant and boastful. In fact, those who are arrogant and boastful are usually cowards (see: compensating). Nor does confidence require you to know all the answers about your life, because you won't. No one does. What it means is looking a challenge in the eye and knowing that, when the dust settles, everything is going to be OK. It means being willing to stand up for what you believe is right and what you believe is best for you, and not giving way to fear. It's an inner peace thing.

OK, it's time for . . .

A Josh Shipp Moment of Vulnerability: A lot of people assume that I'm confident all the time. "Oh yeah, Josh, it's easy for you. You're charismatic. You run your mouth on TV and in front of large audiences. And your hair is always expertly styled." Hair thing? True. Always confident? False. I'll be honest, 50 percent of my life, I'm scared out of my mind. Just like you. I think things like, "They must have the wrong guy—why did they ask ME to do this? I'm not capable of this. This is the big leagues; I don't belong here. I'm not good enough, smart enough, funny enough," etc.

My solution? I call it "pulling a governor." Governors can pretty much do whatever they want because they walk around like they run the place (of course, they actually *do* run the place, but still). They're superconfident and have this natural authority, so no one questions them. No one's like, "What's the governor think he's doing? Who let *him* in here?" He's the governor. He's just like, "What? I'm the governor."

When I was in high school I worked a bit in politics. Being young and being in situations where I felt very much in over my head, I realized something: If you walk into a room or situation totally confident and act like you're SUPPOSED to be there, NO ONE WILL QUESTION YOU. But if you hold back, HESITATE for even a second . . . game over. (Same goes for dancing, by the way. Confidence trumps skill every time.) Basically, it's about getting yourself psyched up, 'cause I've found that you're at your best when you're confident, even if on the inside you're about to wet yourself.

Now, don't be stupid: If you have a question, ask it; if you need help, get it. Being confident doesn't mean being too proud to admit mistakes or ask for input, playing know-it-all, or trying to do everything yourself. Being confident simply means believing that you have what it takes to do the job.

The first few times you try anything you'll be scared. The next few times, a little less scared . . . until one day it comes naturally. But if you walk into your first day on a new job and announce in a panic that you don't even know what you're doing, you're probably not going to get offered a next time. Some people will tell you to "fake it 'til you make it." That's not what I'm telling you. I don't believe in faking it; I believe in believing in yourself. Know this: You have what it takes.

Also, you should know that . . .

// Heroes don't take themselves too seriously

After all this talk about being confident, this might seem out of place. It isn't. Being confident isn't about being perfect. Something I learned early on is you've gotta be willing to laugh at yourself.

Be open and honest about your weaknesses, failures, and mistakes, because you're going to make them (trust me), and other people are going to see it happen (again, trust me). If you run away in embarrassment or pretend you didn't screw up in the first place or blame your mistake on someone else, you're going to get some raised eyebrows.

OK, it's storytime:

Once upon a time I had this really big speech in front of a group of teachers. I'm freaking out for two reasons: (1) It's a really big speech, and (2) I often feel like I don't have anything to say to adults . . . you know, people older than me. I assume (wrongly) that the whole time they're sitting there thinking, "What can this young punk teach me?"

Anyway, it's five minutes before I go on. I do one last bathroom break, go to wash my hands, and while I'm thoroughly scrubbing some water splashes out of the sink—and lands directly on my crotch. Oh joy. Now it appears I have wet myself. There is no way around this. I panic. I tried getting fresh with the hand dryer but there wasn't enough time. My shirt was already untucked and not long enough to cover the darkened watermark.

I have two options in these sorta situations. And so do you.

Option 1: Don't acknowledge it. However, everyone else will notice it and it will distract them.

Option 2: Acknowledge it. Have a good laugh at yourself. Introduce the elephant in the room, and move on.

I opened my speech with the following words: "I'm really glad to be here tonight. Now, I realize everybody says that. But I live it. As you can see I'm so excited to be here tonight I actually wet myself. Don't judge me."

Audience laughs, is no longer distracted by the obvious, and we move on.

Confident people own up when they fail or embarrass themselves. If you're willing to talk about your failures and weaknesses, it's less likely others will use them against you. Most people, if you're open about what you're not good at, will be disarmed by your honesty. Of course, if you're constantly complaining about how you're awful at everything you do, it stops being charming and you start acting like a zombie (more on them in Chapter 11), but if you have a sense of humor and can laugh at your shortcomings, you'll get respect.

The main way to build confidence, though, is to put yourself in new situations and learn. If you hide in your basement all day, the world is going to seem big and bright and scary. And when your parents finally kick you out of their basement and you're forced to emerge, you'll sunburn easily. Very embarrassing. But if you just get out there, you'll become stronger. Look, everyone suffers bouts of self-doubt at times. That's fine. Confidence is about realizing that fact and pressing on anyway.

// Heroes take it on

In a world full of villains, heroes stand up and say, "Bring it on." It's not enough to know who you are and feel confident about what you stand for and what you're trying to do. You can't just talk about being a hero, or just talk about dominating your world. At the end of the day, you've gotta actually get in there and FIGHT.

Now, listen up, 'cause this is critical: Heroes don't fight dirty.

// Heroes play by the rules of the Hero's Creed

"What rules?" you ask.

Well, young grasshopper, there are many . . . but let me break 'em down to two. Heroes are always bound and guided by a strong moral code. This moral code—this determination to use their powers only for good—is what separates the heroes from the villains. We'll call these rules the Hero's Creed. So, if you don't remember anything else from this entire book, remember these two rules— they'll serve you well in your quest for world domination:

1. NO ONE HAS THE RIGHT TO DOMINATE YOUR WORLD.
2. YOU DON'T HAVE THE RIGHT TO DOMINATE ANYONE ELSE'S WORLD.

Let's look at them in detail, shall we?

Number 1: No One Has the Right to Dominate Your World

Please note: People will still TRY. We call those people "villains."

Now, you can GIVE people the right to dominate your world (see: surrender), but that's what wimps, pushovers, common folk, and unremarkably boring people do. You are not one of them.

As a hero, you will not—cannot—stand for other people's attempts to take over your world and control your life. You're driving this Lamborghini. You're writing this story. No one else.

Heroes believe that, ultimately, no one can tell you what to do or how to live. Do heroes still take advice and follow traffic signs? Absolutely—some rules just apply to everyone, all the time, and there's no healthy way to get around them. Laws, for example. But heroes don't automatically accept everything they're told at face value and walk blindly down the path others lay out for them. They think things through, set their own goals, and make their own decisions.

That seems obvious, right? It isn't. The more you go through life, the more you'll have to deal with expectations from others. Some of those expectations will be good things, like living independently and staying out of jail. Some will be negative, like borrowing as much money as you can to buy a house and spending the next thirty years of your life paying for it by holding your nose to the grindstone at a soulless job you hate, or always being suckered into buying the season's "must-have" styles . . . or vintage Batman underwear for $150 (for the record, totally not worth it). You'll need to learn to tell the difference, and act accordingly.

Some of your villains will be people, and their attacks will be very real and very personal. But some of them will be more sneaky, and will attack you by placing expectations or pressures on you. Both of these are ways villains try to dominate your world. Your job is to recognize their schemes, say "no," and stand up and fight.

Number 2: You Don't Have the Right to Dominate Anyone Else's World

If you're going to defend Rule Number 1 and fight for your right to choose your own path and live your own life free from the control of villains, you must give others that same freedom. You can't be a real hero if you're trying to control others on the side. People who dominate others' lives are villains. So if you're going to live like a villain and hurt others, you can't be upset when someone bigger and stronger comes along and beats you down.

Now, here's where this can get tricky: When villains (who don't play by the rules) try to dominate your world, you don't have the right to retaliate. You can't fight evil with evil without becoming evil. To borrow the words of a wise, wrinkled little Jedi master: "Once you start down the dark path, forever will it dominate your destiny."

So, don't go there.

This world-domination thing isn't about you against the world; it's not a competition. You don't have to push people down to build yourself up and dominate the world. You're not Tony Soprano. In fact, dominating your world is about becoming so confident and comfortable with who you are and what you stand for that you're not threatened by anyone else. Which means you'll have plenty of energy left over for helping others dominate their worlds, too (we'll get to that in Part 4).

In the meantime, I owe you a warning: Living by the rules takes courage. Dominating your own world is no simple task. What I'm talking about here is a completely different way of seeing the world and a completely different way of living life. It's going to take work, and you can bet there's going to be opposition.

Prepare to meet your villains.

Part 2

HOW to DOMINATE YOUR VILLAINS

5.

Know Thine Enemy

Get ready for battle.

In the fourth century B.C., there was this brilliant Chinese military leader named Sun-tzu. You gotta understand, this guy pretty much *invented* military strategy, and he explained everything from spy tactics to planning and leading campaigns in a book called *The Art of War*. Remember—this was, like, twenty-five centuries ago, and this dude NAILED it. In fact, *The Art of War* is considered one of the most influential books in history because it inspired so many leaders throughout time, from Napoléon to Mao Zedong to modern-day CEOs.

(Are we the first book for teens to repeatedly mention Napoléon without the last name of "Dynamite"? I believe we are.)

Unfortunately, Sun-tzu's masterpiece focuses quite heavily on breaking Rule Number 2 of the Hero's Creed (he had this thing for dominating other people's worlds), so I can't really recommend it as a "rules to live by" sort of guide. Unless, of course, you want to be a villain, in which case, shame on you, and a plague on your house.

However, *The Art of War* still has a few things to teach those who'd choose the hero's path to world domination. Dominating your world means overcoming obstacles. Some of those obstacles, like rising above bad memories or experiences from your past or getting a decent score on your SATs, are just challenges, right? They don't have feelings or anything. They are things, ideas, and stuff.

Other obstacles—other villains—will come disguised as people. They may be people who don't believe in you or support you, or they may be people who actively try to keep you from reaching your goals and living your own life.

No matter what sort of opponent you face, your first step should be following one of Sun-tzu's primary rules of warfare:

// Know thy enemy

Mr. Sun breaks it down like this:

- If you know your enemies and know yourself, you can win a thousand battles without a single loss.
- If you only know yourself, but not your opponent, you may win or may lose.
- If you know neither yourself nor your enemy, you will always endanger yourself.

Genius, right? Let's examine the lesson here. In Chapter 4, we talked about the importance of confidence, of trusting yourself, of being a hero. If you don't know yourself and what you're capable of, Sun-tzu says every conflict you face will be dangerous, and your enemy will take you down. The man's right.

Confidence alone isn't always enough to succeed, though. If you know yourself, you *might* win . . . and you might lose.

However, if you know yourself and your own limitations AND you know your opponents—if you understand their approach and what they bring to the table—you'll come out on top.

Now, for some sobering news:

// There IS a monster under your bed

Well, maybe not, but there ARE villains in your home, in your school, on your sports teams, among your friends, starring on TV shows, on the Internet, and in your own head. Yes, my friend, villains are real, and they are out to get you.

Before we go further, I think a general definition of villains is in order. In your quest to dominate your world, villains will arise in many different forms. They can appear as thoughts, circumstances, individuals, or ideas. They can be passive, unwitting, or deliberately malicious. But there's one easy way to identify a villain:

> **Villains are anything or anyone that subtracts from you, tears you down, tries to take control, or otherwise distracts you from living your perfect life.**

All villains have this in common.

That said, to really know your enemy you have to be able to do more than simply identify them.

My point is,

// Knowing your enemy requires understanding their point of view

You have to understand what makes your opponents tick.

These days, sometimes that's harder than it sounds. Here's the thing: Even though everyone is so connected through social media, the Internet, and the phones we carry around in our pockets, it's often entirely possible for you to encounter millions of scraps of information on a daily basis, yet never hear a single opinion you disagree with. The problem with this is we begin to see the world in black and white: We are good, and anyone who disagrees with us is bad, and it's that simple.

Only it isn't. It's not enough to know that your enemy's position is different than yours; you have to take time to understand why they've taken that position. Every villain has a backstory—they are who they are because of where they grew up, who their parents were, the experiences they've had, and what they believe about themselves and the world.

When you take an opponent's history into account, it helps you follow the Hero's Creed. First, understanding villains helps you defend against them and keeps them from dominating your world. Second, it helps remind you not to dominate their world.

When you understand your villains, you'll realize two things:

1. There's a little villain in all of us
2. There's a little good in every villain

Allow me to explain. The truth is, we all, at one point or another, behave as villains. We've all hurt someone else's feelings. We've all ignored a friend who needed our help. We've all laughed insensitively at YouTube videos of innocent people injuring themselves and falling into manholes. We've all acted selfishly and destructively at times. No one is exempt. Your dear, sweet grandmother, your best friend—just about anyone can behave villainously at times. However, just because someone is acting like a villain doesn't mean he or she IS a villain. Sometimes people who behave like villains THINK they have good intentions. This is a common problem with robots (more on them in Chapter 9). Sometimes—and I don't mean to scare you here—but even the people you love and trust can say things and act in ways that aren't in your best interests.

But here's the good news: You can usually rescue villains from their villainous ways. This goes for the friend who suddenly starts gossiping about you behind your back and the committed felon on death row.

I'll give you an example: Darth Vader. For the first 99 percent of the Star Wars Trilogy (I'm talking about the originals here . . .

not that abomination with Jar Jar Binks), Darth Vader is the most evil force of destruction in movie history. But Luke Skywalker, his son, is convinced there's still good in him, that he can turn him back from the dark side. Right down to the wire, it seems like Luke is wrong. Then, in the last few moments, Vader turns on the Emperor. He throws him down some bottomless hole (what was that pit doing there, anyway? Talk about a safety hazard) and sacrifices his life to save Luke's.

So in the end, Darth Vader DID have some good in him. He was a good guy who went wrong when he let other villains dominate his world and got sucked into following the wrong crowd (the Emperor) and making bad decisions (hunting Jedi, murdering people, destroying entire planets, and so on). Granted, for a time, his motives were pure evil, and he does some reaaaaalllly bad stuff. My point is, there's hope for everybody.

When we step into the other person's shoes and try to see the world from his or her perspective, we can gain more than victory: We might actually turn a villain into a powerful ally.

Besides, in real life, there are no villains cackling and rubbing their hands together in perverse delight as they contemplate their nefarious (that's for you, dear editor) deeds. There are only people with problems, struggling to solve them as best they know how. The bad guys you'll meet aren't doing bad stuff just so they have an excuse to practice their malevolent laugh and wear dark, hooded garments and crush the happiness of innocent children. It's not that they're just being mean. Villains do bad stuff to get attention, feel better about themselves, or make money. They may be driven by greed, selfishness, or misguided conviction, but in the end, they're people, too, motivated by the same kinds of needs and emotions that drive you and me.

Often the only difference between heroes and villains is that the hero uses his extraordinary powers to help others, while the villain uses his powers for selfish purposes.

Recently, I commissioned the Hey Josh Institute of Knowledge to conduct a study on villains throughout history and modern-day life, and they made an astounding discovery about . . .

// Your life and the seven villains

Think of it like *Snow White and the Seven Dwarfs,* only imagine all the dwarfs are bent on sabotaging your life. (Expect a press release from Disney any day now—it'll make an awesome film.)

Basically, every villain in all of time falls into one of seven distinct classes: Ghosts, ninjas, pirates, robots, vampires, zombies, and puppies.

Yes, puppies.

Let me break it down real quicklike: Ghosts show up to play off your fears and keep you from being a hero. Ninjas seem harmless, but harbor a hidden agenda to take advantage of you. Pirates are just plain bad news—they're out to use you for personal gain. Robots, although sometimes well-meaning, will try to control you and brainwash you with their programming. Vampires look all perfect and awesome, but they'll lure you away from your true self and destroy you. Zombies pull you down with pessimism and negativity. Puppies . . . well, they're great, but they'll blindside you with serious long-term consequences if you're not careful.

So, that's what you're up against.

If you're going to dominate your world, you have to learn to dominate these seven villains. Ready? We'll take 'em on one at a time . . .

6.

Ghosts

Ghosts are possibly the most dangerous villains you'll face, and they're often the hardest to identify, because THEY'RE IN YOUR HEAD. They also team up with nearly all the other villains. If you can dominate your ghosts, all the other villains will be that much weaker.

First, a quick profile:

Ghost

Class—Ghost

Disguises—Painful memories; Bad mistakes; Lies

Mission Statement—To use painful past experiences to damage your present and future opportunities

Signature Moves—Causing fear; Causing doubt; Replaying painful memories; Holding you back; Paralyzing you

How to Defeat Them—Confront them

// Disguises

Ghosts: Don't wear sheets with eyeholes on Halloween. They don't star in movies with Haley Joel Osment and a young (and remarkably creepy) Mischa Barton from *The O.C.* Nope, ghosts show up in your head in the form of painful memories, past mistakes, hurtful words, and lies you've been told (through actions or speech) by other villains, like pirates and ninjas. You know when you're thinking about trying something new or pursuing a goal and you hear a voice in your head telling you that you're not good enough or that you'll never amount to anything or that you'll fail "just like last time"? Ghosts.

In some ways, ghosts are even worse than their reputation.

They are recalled mistakes and regret from missed opportunities. They are the scars left by exes who ditched you for someone else, the discouragement from coaches who told you to give up—that you weren't good enough—and the lingering hurt from classmates who teased you about your appearance, teachers who wrote you off, and parents you never knew or who left when you were young.

// Mission statement

Ghosts are born whenever you suffer injury and feed off bitterness and fear. Ghosts are lingering, lurking liars, and unfortunately, you can't escape them, because they live in your head. I suppose you could escape them if you don't have a head, in which case, I'm curious to know how you're reading this book.

For me, a ghost in my life is my past, especially growing up without my biological family. I'll be honest—at this point, I'm totally cool with it. I go weeks without even thinking about it. I love my life.

However, the ghosts of that hurt still pop up from time to time.

One of these times for me is around the holidays. I don't know, I guess everyone's hanging out with their family, laughing, eating, chugging eggnog, and comparing DNA samples . . . it's like a ghostly reminder whispering, "Hey, Josh, you suck—you don't have real parents. If you weren't such a disappointment maybe they woulda stuck around. But you're all alone."

For a while this would blindside me. September. Great month. October. Great month. November–December? Yeah . . . ouch.

And the bummer thing is, ghosts never leave. They might leave you alone sometimes, but they're always there deep down, whispering lies in your ear. They echo the lies others told you: That you're not smart enough; that you're not pretty; that you'll never amount to anything.

// Signature moves

Ghosts pop up at the worst times. (See above. The holidays? Really?) They show up every time you move forward, every time you take steps toward dominating your world.

It makes sense, though. Why would a ghost speak up if you're loafing around bingeing on Snack Pack pudding? Why would a ghost care if you're dating a jerk? To a ghost, bad decisions just mean more ghost friends, more bad memories, and more ghostly ghostiness. They are the most deceptive of all villains, because they know your weaknesses better than any outside agent.

// How to dominate ghosts

It's tempting to pretend the ghosts aren't there, but picture the ghosts in Super Mario: When you face them, they stop chasing you. Or the ghosts in Pac-Man: Those suckers will keep haunting you until you're strong enough to turn around and eat them. The point is, if you don't deal with ghosts now, they're going to deal with you when you least expect it.

The very reason ghosts are so dangerous—the fact that they are lies inside your head—is also their greatest weakness: You don't have to listen to them. Sometimes their lies are convincing. They lull you back into comfortable ruts, to inaction. They tell you it's not worth it to take risks. Thing is, you can shut them up. Ghosts can't stand up to truth. In the end, they're the only villain you can truly control. If you remember that ghosts are liars, it becomes possible to defeat them.

One of the best things you can do with ghosts is anticipate them. You know, be prepared for them. Hunker down into your best linebacker stance and wait for 'em, then toss 'em to the ground and insult their ghost-mother.

For me, I've learned that when November comes along, I'd best get around my friends and my foster family, and keep myself busy.

Look for patterns—ghosts lack creativity and often repeat themselves.

// How to rescue ghosts

Ghosts are unrepentant villains, and since they aren't people so much as wisps of thought, it's difficult to rescue them from their villainous ways. Ghosts aren't ever going to just straight-up join your side and voluntarily help you. They exist to keep you from dominating your world, and nothing else. However, with the right attitude, you can turn the tables on them and use the lies they whisper to tear you down as a backward compass . . . and take the hurt they've inflicted and use it to help others.

And that's exactly how you can "trick" a ghost into helping you dominate your world. Generally, ghosts like to run their mouths when you're either (a) in a serious funk, or (b) making good decisions, like trying something new or challenging and a little scary but really, really right. If (a), you'll know it; ghosts love to kick you when you're down. So, if you're down and you're getting kicked, stand up and confront the suckers. Use the sting of their lies as fuel for proving them wrong. If (b), take comfort. The fact that your ghosts are giving you such a hard time is proof you're on the right track. The louder and more persistent the ghosts' lies are—the more they try to convince you you're not good enough—the more sure you can be you're following the best path possible. When you stand up for someone being picked on, ghosts will scream, "YOU'LL EMBARRASS YOURSELF!!!" When you date the right guy, ghosts are yelling, "YOU DON'T DESERVE HIM!!!" When you're working hard to follow your dream, ghosts are chattering, "YOU'LL NEVER BE GOOD ENOUGH!!!"

In other words, you can use ghosts as reverse guides. The stronger their lies, the more you know you're on the best road for you. Just do—or believe—the exact opposite of what they're telling you and you'll be alright.

7.

Ninjas

Ninjas are everywhere . . . disguised as friends or skulking in the shadows, waiting for you to drop your guard. You're going along, minding your own business . . . then, suddenly— *shhhunk!!*—you've got a shuriken embedded in your temple. And let me tell you, it's hard to recover from that.

So, if you want to dominate your world and disarm the ninjas before they assassinate you, you gotta know who you're dealing with.

NINJA

Class—Ninja

Disguises—False advertising; Biased media (so, pretty much all media); Greedy corporations; "The Man"; Frenemies

Mission Statement—To appear harmless—even friendly—and earn your trust to fulfill a harmful hidden agenda

Signature Moves—Deception; Bait 'n' Switch; Trickery; Backstabbing; Infiltration; Sabotage

How to Defeat Them—Expose the truth

// Disguises

Like their real-life counterparts, ninjas excel in disguise, stealth, and subterfuge. There are two main types of ninja. The first are corporate ninjas. They're the greedy companies and lying advertisers promising you a better life/bulkier muscles/more dough if you buy their brand just to sell you a product. They're the credit-card companies offering "free" money to ensnare you in a cycle of debt. These are the guys that see a SUCKER stamp plastered across your forehead in glaring red ink. And the worst thing about corporate ninjas? They're so huge—so vast and clever—that they're almost invisible.

The second type hits closer to home. Friend ninjas, commonly known as frenemies, are those friends you trust who unexpectedly whirl around and jab a katana blade deep into your back. They're the "pals" who belittle you or constantly one-up your stories ("Oh, you bought a car? Yeah, my parents are giving me a Mercedes when I graduate . . .") to tear you down. Frenemies are really just a lesser form of pirate, so we'll talk more about them in Chapter 8.

// Mission statement

Ninjas are tricky, of course. On the surface, ninjas appear to be on your side. They have a way of interacting with you that at first glance seems completely normal. But after a while (usually not until after they've launched an attack), you realize that their agenda is either to rip you apart or to take advantage of you.

Ready for some bummer news? Ninjas are generally awesome at what they do. They're highly skilled and, let's be honest, they look pretty cool, too. But their entire purpose in life is to sneak in and destroy. Ninjas have no honor. They crouch in the shadows or dress up like your new kitten. They wait 'til you're at your most vulnerable. Then they strike—like a coward—from the shadows when your back is turned.

// Signature moves

Ninjas seem completely innocent, but before you know it, *wham!* they have destroyed your self-esteem, confidence, mood, or all three. How do they do it? By gaining and then taking advantage of your trust. They pretend to be on your side. They say they have your best interests at heart.

Picture those Axe Body Spray commercials. If you're a guy, Axe promises you'll have hot girls running down the street after you and biting off your arm like you're made of chocolate. Wow, Axe! You'd do that for me? That's really nice of you. . . .

Really, though, Axe wants your money. And to get it from you, they'll first remind you of your ghosts (usually the ones kicking around your brain making you feel insecure or inferior) and then subliminally promise to make those ghosts go away . . . if you just buy their product. You think Axe cares if you ever get a date? Trust me, Axe has no stake in anything but the precious little dollars from your skanky little mitts. And to add insult to injury, Axe doesn't even deliver! It just makes you stink like a junior high boy trying too hard to be cool. I would know.

Credit-card companies love to pull the same stunt: They send you a "preapproved" plastic card in the mail that magically allows you to buy whatever you want RIGHT NOW! And there's apparently no risk whatsoever. Only an idiot would pass that up, right? Well, pretty soon, your credit score is shot, you're $20K in debt, and your own mother won't lend you a buffalo nickel. What happened? The ninja tricked you: He promised you instant gratification and the power to buy things that would make you feel better about yourself or impress other people . . . and, with the help of your ghosts, he convinced you that he really wanted to help. So, you took the bait . . . and swallowed the poison.

Maybe you've got a new friend and she seems caring and kind, but then embarrassing pictures of you start getting texted to everyone you know, and your "friend" is making out with your boy-friend every time you blink. Hate to break it to ya, but your "friend" is a ninja.

// How to dominate ninjas

Now for some good news. For all their sneaky skills and silent weapons, ninjas don't stand a chance in an open fight. There's a reason ninjas hide in the shadows and attack you from behind: *You're stronger than they are.* Ninjas can hurt you only if you let them past your guard, and the only way past your guard is by tricking you into thinking that they aren't a threat.

That's why a door-to-door salesman ninja might not even make it inside—you see what his game is right away, so you're much less likely to be taken advantage of. But advertising ninjas, attacking through TV, billboards, and magazines, can convince you your life is empty if you don't employ the right lip gloss or wear the right clothes. If a conniving would-be ninja "friend" shows up and starts bad-mouthing you in front of your other friends right away, her cover is blown . . . so instead, she worms her way into your circle and starts spreading rumors, gradually turning everyone else against you. You know you're dealing with a friend ninja when you hear the phrase "I love her to death, but . . ."

FRENEMY PHRASES TO WATCH OUT FOR
"SHE'S COOL, BUT..."
"NOT TO BE A JERK, BUT..."
"DON'T TELL HER I SAID THIS, BUT..."

But here's the thing: Ninjas can't survive if you know who they are and what they're doing. They need shadows. Ergo, you need light.

Try not to become a paranoid cynic or conspiracy theorist, but DO try to test everything. (Thinking = very valuable skill; practice often.) With corporation ninjas, that means simply being aware of what their game is. Remember, corporations and brands want you to like them and buy their stuff, so they'll do whatever they can to try to appeal to you and convince you that they are what you want. That's their agenda. YOUR JOB is to figure out for yourself whether or not you want them. You have to decide if what they're offering you is actually something you need, instead of simply letting them control you with their tricky persuasive messages. Maybe that new Volcano Steak Guacamole Chipotle Burrito Pizza looks appealing at 1 A.M. on a Saturday night, but if you know it's just going to tear apart your intestines like a rabid wolverine, you're less likely to cave in.

Friend ninjas are more tricky. Sometimes you won't even see the attack until it's too late. Your best chance is to be upfront when you suspect ninja tactics. If you suspect your new friend is trying to sabotage you or use you to get to something else they want, call him out. You don't have to be a villain about it and bust a cap in 'em or anything, but if you let friend ninjas know you're onto them, you're paying attention, and you won't stand for it, they'll back off. Remember, they generally know they don't stand a chance in an open fight.

// How to rescue ninjas

Remember, there's a little good in every villain. A lot of times, unfortunately, corporation ninjas (as an entity) don't care about anything except money. But they also really really want people to like them. If people don't like them, they don't make money. So if a corporation or brand is going all crazy ninja and really taking advantage of people, call 'em out. Send them some feedback explaining how they lost your respect (and your business) and threaten to expose them as the villain they are to all your friends. If enough people hold them accountable, it's possible to convert ninja corporations into corporate do-gooders.

Oh man, I feel a story coming on . . .

OK, check it out: In 2005, McDonald's launched a banner campaign featuring a young dude drooling over a double cheeseburger. "Double cheeseburger? I'd hit it. I'm a dollar menu guy," said the animated ad. Complaints ensued about the sexual nature of the ad (um, "I'd hit it"?) and McDonald's pulled the ad, claiming that their marketing department misunderstood the term. Thank you, McDonald's, for associating double cheeseburgers with hooking up. Please never do that again.

A more positive example would be something like Ben & Jerry's. When a consumer discovered that the ice cream manufacturers didn't have her specific flavor choice available—banana ice cream with fudge and walnut chunks—she wrote in specifically to request it. *Boom:* Chunky Monkey was born. This is how history is made, kids.

Your chances of rescuing friend ninjas (or any other ninja-like individual) from their villainous ways are better, but still slim. Here's the key: Be a samurai. Samurais are everything ninjas wish they were, and most important, samurais have *honor.* They don't resort to tricks and deception to get what they want. Odds are, friend ninjas are jealous of you to begin with—a lot of times that's what's driving them to tear you down. If you treat friend ninjas kindly no matter what they do, they may start to look up to you and realize that their tactics don't work. Again, shine the light on what they're doing and call it like it is: A cowardly attempt to take advantage of someone else. But instead of just shaming them, accept them (a lot of times, that's all they're after, anyway) and teach them how to be a hero. That way, everybody wins. (Cue studio audience going "Awwww.")

8.

Pirates

Pirates are easy to spot, even when they're not wearing eye patches, brandishing long curved swords, and shouting *"Argh!"* Some pirates are gnarly looking, others are really attractive, but ALL OF THEM leave a trail of destruction floating in their wake.

Here's what to look for.

Pirate

Class—Pirate

Disguises—Bullies; Psycho boyfriends; Criminals

Mission Statement—To get what they want by taking advantage of you

Signature Moves—Threatening; Coercing; Exploiting; Destroying; Stealing

How to Defeat Them—Get away!

// Disguises

Pirates are brazen jerks. You know how ninjas are all sneaky-like in their attempt to take advantage of you? Yeah, pirates aren't subtle like that. Pirates come in many forms, but they all want the same thing: What THEY want, at your expense. From terrorists and warlords to controlling boyfriends who pressure you to sleep with them, a pirate wants to pillage you to get what he or she wants.

// Mission statement

Pirates care about one thing: Themselves. Pirates wreak havoc on other people's lives because, to a pirate, nothing matters but the loot. You are either a tool for a pirate to use or an obstacle a pirate must crush. They will commandeer your life and sail it right into a cliff.

// Signature moves

Pirates lie, cheat, and steal to get what they want. When that doesn't work, they're happy to get violent. They threaten, abuse, rape, kill, and plunder—they are the most obviously destructive villains in the crew. A bully might threaten you with physical harm to control you. A Wall Streeter might lie and cheat and race off with all your savings. A pirate can mess with your life in a million different ways, and trust me, none of them are good.

// How to dominate pirates

There is one foolproof way to dominate pirates: Steer clear of them. If you're paying attention, you'll see pirates coming a long way off. Pirates aren't subtle. Sometimes you need to trust your instincts. If someone seems off when you meet him, chances are you're detecting a pirate. If a person is constantly cracking jokes at others' expense, or wielding his dominant personality as a battering ram to hurt others, chances are he'll do the same to you.

Sometimes pirates have a sort of loud, powerful personality that's appealing. After all, living a life on the high seas, partying, and plundering for a living does have its charms, and a pirate will play the role of loyal friend if it means that he can use you. But the moment you assert yourself—the moment you try to be a hero and dominate your own world—pirates get pissed. If you play by their rules, they'll keep you around. Things might even seem fun for a while. But if you try to live your own life, the relationship might get dangerous. If a pirate doesn't drag you into trouble with him, in the end he'll discard you like a booger-ridden bandana.

Do yourself a favor and run.

Look, this might sound easy enough, but sometimes it's actually really hard to turn away. 'Cause pirates love to pick fights. Talk trash. Make fun of your mom. Carry a chip on their shoulder (typically their left shoulder—the right shoulder is usually reserved for their parrot. Or some other creature. Perhaps a young duck).

For example, in 2005, I was asked to become a spokesperson for National Foster Care Month. As a former foster kid, I was honored. I couldn't wait to speak to young people about foster care. I felt like in some small way I'd be giving back to a system that has given so much to me.

Well, this social worker dude in Oklahoma who works in the foster care system heard about this great honor that had been bestowed upon me and said, "Oh, Josh Shipp. Ha! I know him. He was such a punk kid—probably still is a punk kid. I can't believe they asked *him* to do that. What a joke!"

Excuse me? No you didn't. Tell me you did NOT just say that about me.

Pretty offensive, right? So listen carefully. I would now like to give you that man's full name and e-mail address. Your mission, should you choose to accept it, is to send him hate mail. Cyberbully the crap out of him until he despises his very life.

I'd like to do that . . . but it's not the right thing to do. It's not the hero thing to do. And it's just plain wrong to retaliate like that. Remember what I said earlier, you can't confront villains with your own villainous behavior.

Ah, forget it—e-mail me and I'll give his info to you. I'm joking.

No, I'm not.

Yes, I am.

Now that we're both confused . . .

Honestly, when I heard about this dude's comment, I was pissed. I wanted to pick up the phone and chew him out. I wanted to start a Web site called www.<Guy's Full Name>isatotaljerkand hismomhasabeard.com.

I wanted to make him look like a fool. I wanted to see if I had enough power to get him fired.

But this is exactly what a pirate wants. A fight. They want to get your attention, distract you. Pull you down to their level. Smack you around a bit to make themselves feel more powerful and important. And maybe ruin your reputation while they're at it.

It's not worth it. Sometimes all you want to do is throw a punch or start a nasty rumor to get revenge, but the saying's a lie—revenge isn't sweet. It makes you feel like a jerk. You end up no better than they are . . . plus you end up stuck in a cycle of mutually assured destruction. Trench warfare ensues. No one wins.

The best move? Write them off. Tune them out. Focus on the 90 percent of people in your life that DO support you, not the 10 percent trying to tear you to pieces for sport.

Surround yourself with people who see you for who you COULD BE, not who you were.

So, what do you think of that, Mr. Oklahoma Social Worker? Not bad advice, you know . . . coming from a "punk kid" and all.

// How to rescue pirates

When people care only about themselves, there's not much you can do. That doesn't mean that there isn't hope for pirates; some pirates will get older, regret the havoc they've wreaked, and start to amend their villainous ways.

But as long as they are pirates . . . as long as they've got those hook hands and eye patches and beards with crumbs stuck in them . . . as long as they carry catastrophe everywhere they go—stay away. There's no reasoning with pirates. All they'll do is hurt you, and the best you can do is avoid them completely, warn your friends, and hope that someday these pirates can be honest citizens.

9.

Robots

Robots are particularly interesting, because they aren't always bad. In fact, some robots may have your best interests in mind. Think about R2D2, or WALL-E. Or think about Arnold Schwarzenegger as the Terminator, who was sent to kill Sarah Connor in the first *Terminator* movie, but is sent to protect her son in the second and third. In short, robots do whatever they are programmed to do. If they're programmed to be your loyal sidekick, you're set.

At the same time, robots may be the most dangerous enemy you'll face. They are strong. They are made of metal. They think entirely with cold, calculated reason. With a robot, there is no underdog, no tenacity, no wits. A robot just is. If a robot is not programmed to help you, you are in a bind. Just ask Sarah Connor. (Actually, you can't. She's a fictional character, not a real person. But you know what I mean.)

Because of that strength and machinelike calculation, you'll face a lot of robots on your way to dominating your own world. School can sometimes seem like one big robot factory, churning out new models so they can be programmed in robot school (college), then go to work in robot command centers (office buildings), separated by cubicles structured in precise right angles to maximize efficiency.

Here's what you need to know about robots.

Class—Robot

Disguises—Overbearing parents; Bitter teachers; Closed-minded counselors; Petty managers

Mission Statement—To conform themselves and others to pre-established expectations and follow set orders unquestioningly

Signature Moves—Controlling; Pressuring; Conforming; Living their dreams through you; Programming you to be like them

How to Defeat Them—Create your own plan

// Disguises

Robots are everywhere. They show up at home, at school, in the workplace, as costars in Will Smith action movies, and in certain electronics stores (have you SEEN those self-propelled vacuum things?!). Most often, robots will turn up as well-meaning but misguided grown-ups—parents, teachers, and coaches can all act like robots from time to time.

// Mission statement

If you saw any of those *Terminator* movies, then you know what robots are about. They are steel-strong and relentless. They carry out their work tirelessly, without complaint and without compromise. When they have a mission to fulfill, they will carry out that mission if it's the last thing they do. Robots are good at what they do. Otherwise they'd be useless, and a useless robot gets sent to the trash heap.

The thing with robots is, they do only what they are programmed to do. They do what they are taught is right. Needless to say, this quality can be incredibly irritating. Take WALL-E. WALL-E was programmed for waste management, and WALL-E would likely ask you to spend a day cleaning trash with him. He'd assume this would be great fun for you, because that's what's great fun to him. If you yelled at WALL-E and said, "I hate picking up garbage!" he wouldn't understand. There's nothing wrong with the way he's programmed, and it's not good or bad. It's just who WALL-E is.

Your parents can be the same way. They may believe you should be a doctor or a lawyer. To them, these are careers successful people follow, and they want you to be successful. There's nothing wrong with becoming a doctor, but maybe that's not what you want. If you scream, "I don't want to be a doctor!" they won't understand. They want what they think is best for you. They were trained and programmed a certain way, and don't understand that you might be programmed differently.

// Signature moves

Is all hope lost? All hope is not lost.

Most robots are subconsciously programmed to dominate your world. Because they're programmed to believe that what they do and think is the only acceptable path, they become very concerned when other people choose a different path—when others think or act in ways that run against robots' programming. So robots interfere and do everything they can to turn you into one of them. It's not exactly an evil intention, just a mistaken one. Given their way, robots will replace your human limbs with robot arms and legs until finally you are programmed to their liking and you work your nine-to-five job quietly and efficiently, earning robot credits (money) so you can buy a better robot transportation module (car) and pay for robot relaxation time marine excursions (cruises).

Those things aren't awful in themselves, but trust me: You don't want to be a robot. Why? Because robots do not dominate their world. *Robots are completely and utterly dominated by their programming*—whether it's from their parent-robots or the forces and systems of culture and "the way things work," also known by such code names as "common sense" or "tradition." They have no choice; robots do the bidding of others. And once you've been programmed, you stop caring about your dreams and goals. You start caring more about earning robot credits to pay the robot bills. Your work has meaning only because the program tells you it does.

And what kind of life is that?

// How to dominate robots

It's tempting to stand up against robots, to fight them tooth and nail to try and keep them from programming you. It's tempting to take them on directly. But robots are too powerful to attack head-on. If you trip a robot's "threat" sensors or identify yourself as an enemy, you are in big, big trouble.

Fortunately, there's a way to beat robots. In the end, it's not even that hard. You just have to understand how robots work.

Like so many other villains, the robot's greatest weakness lies in what makes them so dangerous: Programming. If a robot isn't programmed to destroy you, if it's programmed to help you instead, the game is changed. Suddenly, you've got all that power and metal working for you. 'Cause here's the thing: Robots can be some of the greatest allies you'll ever find.

Robots operate on logic and reason. To a robot, there is only one way, and that one way is how they were programmed. For instance, if you play sports, you might deal with a coach-bot. Coach-bots care about their sport. They don't care if you have to study, or send in college applications or sleep. They care about soccer or football or volleyball or softball. The same goes for teach-bots, or counsel-bots or parent-bots. If you say, "This is stupid. I don't care about soccer (or algebra or history)!" the coach-bot will respond in a robot-programmed voice, "Does not compute. Sports teach valuable life lessons about teamwork, strength, and winning. I love soccer. You should also love soccer." This is where the arguments begin. I'm guessing you've had one or two of these, especially with your parents.

You should've heard the robots when I blurted out as a seventeen-year-old class clown that I wanted to be a motivational speaker. "You'll live in a van down by the river! Is that really a job? You'll be homeless and smell of Doritos! What a joke! You can't even motivate yourself to get good grades! Oh, look at Mr. Motivator!" Their processors were jammed. They were brutal. They desperately wanted me to follow their pre-approved paths for success.

The most crushing comment came from a career-adviser robot, which is someone who, I assume, is supposed to advise you in your career. (Just reading through the lines here.)

"Well, that's sweet, Josh." (She said it like polite Southern women say, "Bless your heart," when what they really mean is, "You're such an idiot.")

"That's nice and all but . . . you need to have a backup plan."

Thanks, lady. You could've just said, "Good for you, but you're gonna fail. You might as well embrace that now!"

How do you deal with that? How do you deal with someone telling you that you can't do something?

I'll tell you what I did. Bear in mind this isn't traditional advice and would probably make Dr. Phil shake his head and say, "Now, now, young man. Take it easy."

But I told you I'd be honest, so here it is. What I did, when my personal robots told me I was off the reservation and couldn't succeed unless I followed their standard plan and met their traditional expectations, was I just took everyone's disbelief and their total lack of confidence in me and used it as fuel to move me forward.

"I'll show them," I thought to myself. "One day they'll take back those words!"

Looking back, I was probably motivated more by pride than anything really noble.

I'm not saying it's the BEST long-term plan. But it can work.

Really, you've gotta do what works for you. And what works for you may be different from what works for me. The key is not letting the robots discourage you from pursuing your goals. And to do that, you need to have a plan.

(It probably wouldn't hurt to have a little humility, too.)

Now, it's tempting when trying to argue with a robot to get all emotional—scream or cry or grumble or whatever—because sometimes robots seem unreasonable. But getting all emotional on a robot is a bad idea for two reasons: (1) robots don't understand emotions; and (2) robots are actually EXTREMELY reasonable. You simply need to speak in their language and convince the robot that your choice, your preference, your life goal, is logical.

Here's how this works. Or rather, how this DOESN'T work. Let's imagine you're having a discussion with your robot guidance counselor based purely on the emotions raging through your mind. You two are sitting in her office; there's a poster of some kittens on the wall and a bowl of hard candies that has not been touched or otherwise altered in three decades sitting on the table. Scene:

> ***Counsel-bot 2000:*** *Where would you like to go to college?*
>
> ***You:*** *Actually, I don't want to go to a typical college. I want to go to photography trade school because I love photography.*
>
> ***Counsel-bot 2000:*** *That sounds lovely. Perhaps you can take a photography class at college. I see here that your grades in math and science are low. In order to get into a great college you really need to improve your scores in these areas to become a well-rounded student and individual.*
>
> ***You:*** *Math and science are stupid. Screw that crap. College is dumb and overrated. Are we done yet?*
>
> ***Counsel-bot 2000 (with big sad WALL-E cartoon robot eyes):*** *What? Of course you should care! How could you not see how important this is in your life? (Then you argue and mentally check out of the relationship. Every interaction from this point on becomes a battle, not about your career but about whether or not you will accept the counsel-bot's programming.)*

// Hmm. That didn't work out too well, did it?

It's not that you were wrong. It's that you didn't explain things in robot terms. So, let's try again, this time using logic:

> **Counsel-bot 2000:** *Where would you like to go to college?*
>
> **You:** *Actually, I don't want to go to a typical college. I want to go to photography trade school because I love photography.*
>
> **Counsel-bot 2000:** *That sounds lovely. Perhaps you can take a photography class at college. I see here that your grades in math and science are low. In order to get into college, you really need to improve your scores in these to become a well-rounded student and individual.*
>
> **You:** *I have decided that I would really like to pursue photography considering my grades in high school were strongest in this area. Since I do not plan to make a career in the fields of math and science, I would like to pursue my area of greatest strengths first to see if it's a good fit. My plan is to save up enough money to attend a one-year photography trade school that focuses on all aspects of the photography industry and business. If I end up not liking it, I will have lost only one year and would then know it's in my best interests to move on.*

***Counsel-bot 2000 (smiling blankly because robots
often think they are clever, but rarely are):*** *Yes, but
you'll need to learn math and science to run a photography
business.*

You: *Yes, you are correct, but running a photography
business based on math and science will do me no good
unless I am actually a good photographer. No amount of
textbook long division and physics can help me take better
pictures. When I have experience in photography and
know I want to do this forever, I'll have plenty of time to
learn the appropriate math required to run a successful
business if I choose to go that route.*

***Counsel-bot 2000 (confused that you have thought
this through so clearly):*** *What is your backup plan?
(P.S. They always ask this if you outsmart them or provide
logical reasoning for something they don't like.)*

You: *Backup plans are for people who are scared of failure
and don't think they can succeed. I don't plan on just giving
up on my goal because it's hard. Photography is what I want
to do and I will work at it until I have succeeded as a
photographer or found something else that gets me even more
excited. Neither of those options require a backup plan.*

// Congratulations! You just dominated a robot.

Ta-da! As you can see, robots do not respond well to emotion. What
they respect is programming. For all their faults, robots understand

that others are programmed differently. All you have to do is devise your own program—know who you are, what you want, and why—and be able to articulate it rationally. Promise, it's not that tricky.

In the example above, you already created your own plan regarding photography school. Robots love plans! You methodically thought through the results of your actions, and arranged your time and life priorities in the right order to accomplish the plan. This personal programming didn't allow for the counsel-bot 2000 to download its programming into you. Success! You defeated Counsel-bot 2000!

Here's the lesson. If you don't have your own programming in place, it's that much harder to counteract robots looking to copy their programming onto you. If you take the time to develop your own programming, robots respect will that.

But why do we even have to deal with these robots? Because, like mosquitoes and bad haircuts, the world is filled with them. In fact, the world needs them. In the sense that we all have programming, at some level we're ALL robots. Besides, someone has to do data entry. The best part about robots goes back to *Terminator*. When they're against you, good luck. They're remorseless, relentless, and strong. But when you can turn them to your side, you have a valuable ally, a force willing to fight for you and help you accomplish your goals. Once Counsel-bot 2000 understands your programming, it will follow its own programming and work to get you into that trade school, and Counsel-bot 2000 has access to tools and advice you wouldn't have otherwise. After all, it's what they are programmed to do.

See what I mean? All it took was understanding how robots think and turning them into your ally.

// How to rescue robots

It's important to remember that robots are an integral part of society. A necessity. You can't avoid them or eliminate them, so learning to turn them to your side is vital. Consider it a basic life skill like washing a dish or avoiding elastic-waist jeans after the age of ten. If you know how to deal with them, robots are mostly harmless. Robots dominate your world because it's what they've been programmed to do, and usually they earnestly believe they're doing you a favor. If you have a friend or parent or teacher who's behaving like a robot—unwittingly trying to control other people and dictate their lives for them—one thing you can try to do is update their programming. Robots don't naturally understand non-robots, and often get really frustrated when people act different from the way they themselves have been programmed. But it's possible that you can get a robot to understand and respect other people's differences and to stop trying to copy its code onto other people's hardware by explaining (rationally, logically) the benefits of listening to other people and understanding their points of view before asking (or demanding) to be understood.

Remember, robots respect logic. To make a robot your ally, you need to communicate your plan clearly and reasonably. If you communicate a clear, reasonable plan, a robot will see you are an intelligent, reasonable being. Once a robot understands, you have a valuable sidekick. When they're not trying to kill you, robots love to help.

10.

Vampires

Before *Twilight* and all its sequels, knock-offs, and me-too vampire stories took over popular culture, vampires were bad. Like, awful-stuff-of-nightmares bad. They were not attractive teenagers with soulful eyes and lightly tousled hair. Think about it: Vampires were originally impossibly strong, immortal, undead monsters that hunted people at night and sucked all their blood out of their bodies. Gross, right? Now, I'm sure some of them are alright; this Edward fella even seems like kind of a heroic dude (more on him later). The original vampire, though, was Count Dracula, and his character was based on Vlad the Impaler, an actual historical figure with a terrifying mustache who killed around 80,000 people in the 1400s in sick, sick ways.

Know this: While the vampires trying to dominate your world aren't crazy murderers, they're still dangerous.

First, a quick profile:

Vampire

Class—Vampire

Disguises—Trashy celebrities; Addictions; Negative influencers

Mission Statement—To draw you in and steal your identity

Signature Moves—Luring; Enticing; Seducing; Empty promises

How to Defeat Them—Self-esteem

// Disguises

Vampires are anything you can't resist and anyone you wish you were. Like ghosts, the danger from vampires comes largely from within you. Unlike ghosts, however, vampires aren't in your head— they are the people society puts on a pedestal, and the stuff you (falsely) believe you need to be happy. They are drugs. They are alcohol. They are supermodels and starting quarterbacks, gorgeous actresses and hip rock stars. Some of them look like Megan Fox. One of them actually IS Megan Fox. Sometimes, however, they aren't even that famous or popular. Sometimes they're just the people we see and think, "I want to be like that." When we think that, we've been bitten.

// Mission statement

Vampires are superpopular, mysterious, charming, and powerfully seductive. Although you might suspect from time to time that something's a little off, they seem to have it all together. In fact, they seem . . . better than you. Naturally superior. They drive better cars, wear nicer clothes, have cuter boyfriends, and do cooler things on the weekends . . . oh, and also? They know it. Fact is, you're jealous. You're envious. Vampires make you believe who you are and what you have isn't good enough; that you'd be happier "if only . . ."

Drugs and alcohol work the same way. They pull you in with powerful empty promises—if you drink this or inject that or sniff this up your nose, then you'll feel better about yourself . . . escape your pain . . . be accepted . . . respected . . . mature . . . more fun . . . more interesting . . . more creative . . . free from the rules . . .

Vampires spot your own insecurities and influence your desires against you to manipulate you.

// Before you know it, they start to suck your blood

Now of course there may not be actual blood removal; remember, this is a metaphor. But they start to drain you of your independence and your identity until you are just like them . . . or completely dependent upon them. Once bitten by a vampire's charm or beauty, you start to change. It starts with something as little as a new shirt—you know, one more along the lines of the one the vampire is wearing. Six months later, the only way people can tell you apart is she's the one telling the jokes, and you're the one laughing at them. Before you know it, you've forgotten who you used to be. Vampires suck away your identity until you're a carbon copy of them. Soon you're telling those same weak jokes, you're at the same parties, and you can't even remember who you're supposed to be.

If the vampire is lucky, you won't even realize how much you've actually changed before you start trying to "bite" others.

Vampires promise you fame and status and popularity . . . at the cost of yourself. Ever seen the movie *Mean Girls* with Lindsay Lohan? My point exactly. Ever consider what becoming "famous" did to Lindsay as a person? Again, my point exactly.

With substance abuse, it's the same way. Sure, you might feel better when you're under the influence, but the "change" isn't real. But it's tricked you . . . and it has teeth that won't let you go. Before you know it, the vampires control you. You're an addict. A junkie. A burnout. Bottom line? You're dominated. You're at the vampire's mercy.

Oh, and you could overdose and die. And that's NOT a metaphor.

The issue with things like this is that they will never, ever, ever be enough. We think, "When I get this, THEN I'll be happy." Or, "When I get that, THEN I'll be content."

Don't believe it. Don't lie. You know this isn't true. You know what happens: You get whatever it is you wanted, and yeah, it's cool for a few weeks . . . but then it's just an iPod, just a sweatshirt, just a skate deck, just a car, just a job, just a relationship with its normal challenges. You're back where you started.

Sometimes vampires seem completely harmless at first. Like poker. I love poker. (Did you know it's sport now? I mean, it's on ESPN and everything.)

When Texas Hold'em blew up and became superpopular, I admit I found myself watching a lot of those late-night tourneys. The final table. The pocket rockets. The bad beat. The flush. The river. I knew all the lingo.

It looked pretty easy to me. And it was kind of glamorous,

you know. These superchill hot shot guys sitting around a table, playing cards, and winning piles of cash. I wanted to be a part of the action. So, I decided that I would play online. You know, just with PRETEND money.

It was a rush for a while, but eventually that just wasn't exciting enough. That didn't get the pulse in my neck going. I got greedy.

So I signed up to play for real money. Just $100. Which turned to $1,000. Then $10,000.

I was totally and completely hooked. I mean, I guess I always knew I have sort of an addictive personality, but I told myself I wasn't one of *those* guys. I wasn't so easily hooked. I'm no idiot.

Ummm . . . yes I am. I was a total idiot.

It consumed me. I would go to bed thinking about how I should have played hands differently. How I could have won. It affected my health, my friends, my relationships, my work, my showering habits.

It really is amazing how something like this can sneak up on you. One day it's just an innocent little thing. Next moment? *Boom.* You're hooked. You're addicted.

I was addicted and this gambling vampire owned me and was sucking away my identity.

It wasn't until I hit rock bottom (which for me meant losing piles of cash and ruining a lot of relationships) that I woke up and thought, What the crap am I doing? Is this really how I wanna spend my life? Gambling? Online?

Lame.

I kept this a secret for a long time. I wouldn't tell anybody. I would hide in my office for four to five hours at a time and secretly gamble. I think it hit me how pathetic I was when my friend Jason came over to tell me that his wife was pregnant, but I was in the middle of playing a hand.

Get this: I didn't even stop playing to listen to his news. Didn't shake his hand. Didn't hug him, congratulate him . . . nothing.

What kind of jerk does that?!?

Gambling made me a jerk. Am I really a jerk? No. But when vampires attack us and start controlling us they can cause us to do things that aren't normally in our personality.

It's embarrassing to even write about this. It makes me look weak and stupid. But I have to share this with you because, right now, as you read this, some of you are being CONTROLLED by a vampire in your life.

If something has gripped you, you need to put it in a head-lock. It's time for you to stop the bleeding.

// How to dominate vampires

There is one and only one way to escape a vampire: Fight back. Expose it. Tell someone.

"But I don't want to." Fine. I hope you like slavery.

"But it's embarrassing." Doesn't matter. Having your life suck because some vampire *owns* you is MORE embarrassing.

"I'll tell someone tomorrow." Liar.

"I can defeat this on my own." Really? How's that been going for ya?

"This is normal." No, it's not.

In the end, I broke down. Seriously. I was a mess. I was literally crying—snot flying everywhere, ego crushed. It was one of the scariest things ever to tell someone, but it was, without question, the first step to kicking that vampire's tail.

Once you've been bitten, you need help to escape.

What's the best solution to escaping the trap of vampires? Never get bit in the first place.

'Cause here's the thing: Vampires can't force you to change or to become one of them. For all their strength, vampires can't actually hurt you . . . unless you let them. They pour all their energy into making themselves appealing, attractive, persuasive, and seductive. They exert incredible *pressure* on people, coaxing them to give in.

They can say you'd be better off wearing boots covered in mink fur farm-raised in a Siberian village. They can assure you a tribal tattoo is still unique, and you should spend more time lifting weights than reading great books. They can beckon you from the cover of *Glamour,* promising more attention if you showed more cleavage. They can suggest you'll be more interesting or desirable or manly if you got high on the weekends and drank 'til you puked on your overpriced shoes.

You can't escape the vampires' voices. But check it out: You can *ignore* them. Ultimately, it's your choice whether or not you get bitten. It's your choice to stay who you are or become someone else; to control your own life or become a slave to something. Your greatest weapon in the battle against vampires isn't garlic, stakes, or a crucifix, but simply this: Contentment. If you're happy with who you are and what you have, the vampires have nothing to offer.

// How to rescue vampires

Drug vampires and other addictive substances are pretty much irredeemable (look it up if you have to). You've heard the expression "Everything in moderation"? Yeah, doesn't apply here. Just stay away and save yourself the pain.

People vampires, on the other hand . . . sometimes they're the most innocent of all villains. Remember, some of these vampires are just normal people. Sure, they may be extremely popular, wildly successful, or heartbreakingly beautiful, but most of the time, it's your own obsession with becoming LIKE them that makes these people villains in your life. Sometimes the best way to "rescue" a vampire is to give yourself an attitude check. Don't envy; be happy. If you've got your own stuff together, these good people with vampire potential could be loyal friends and valuable allies.

Take Edward and the Cullens from *Twilight*. They know they're alluring and attractive and have the power and potential to destroy. I mean, they ARE vampires, after all. But they restrain themselves. They don't try to force other people to become like them. They don't look down on regular humans and make them feel inferior. Instead, they use their position on the pedestal to set a good example to other vampires and help humans.

Other times, people vampires know the seductive power they wield and use it to draw you in and ensnare you. Not cool. These are the "friends" who accept you only if you like and do the same things they do. Know this: These vampires are just poseurs. Really,

really insecure poseurs. If you find them impressive or attractive, I've got advice for you: Raise your standards. World-dominating heroes are SO better than that.

The point is, you are you, and you're only going to be happy being you. I know that's clichéd, but it's clichéd because it's true. Everyone respects those who are confident and secure in who they are. The people who obsess about clothes and beauty, who are constantly worried about keeping up and fitting in . . . they aren't happy. Don't let the vampires lure your into their trap.

11.

Zombies

Ah, zombies . . . those slow, stupid, terrifyingly ugly, reanimated corpses that get blown away by the bushel with shotgun blasts in every B-grade horror flick. Now, I'm not talking about the Olympic sprinter zombies in *28 Days Later* and *Left 4 Dead*. Those freakishly fast zombies had too much Red Bull or something. I'm talking about the old-school zombies—the creepy, slothful brain-eaters.

In your world, they look something like this:

Class—Zombie

Disguises—Debbie Downers; Chronic complainers; Conspiracy theorists; Pessimists

Mission Statement—To drag you down by focusing on the worst in every situation

Signature Moves—Complaining; Whining; Nagging; Gossiping

How to Defeat Them—Gratitude

// Disguises

We all know zombies in real life. They're the people who stagger through their waking life, complaining to anyone who will listen about how awful life is. Maybe they don't actually have a strand of drool dangling from the corner of their mouth and a chunk of flesh stuck between their decaying teeth, but generally they're easy to recognize. They're that kid who never smiles, that teacher who openly hates her job, that friend who finds a cloud in every silver lining. Those girls who can never find anything nice to say? Who always stand around comparing horror stories about how awful their lives are? Yeah, they're zombies.

// Mission statement

Zombies are the most depressing, pessimistic, and consistently negative people around. Imagine a bad mood wrapped in a rainy day stuck in a moldy basement, and you pretty much have the gist of a zombie. They moan and whine with remarkable persistence: There's nothing on TV, lunch tastes like barf, this movie sucks, your friends are lame. To a zombie, nothing is ever good enough.

You know the saying "Misery loves company"? With zombies, it's true—they're always looking for someone on whom they can bestow their baggage. The more people listen, the more negativity is spread, and the more souls are infected.

// Signature moves

At first, zombies don't seem like a big deal, They're slow and they're dumb. They walk weird. You can easily outrun them.

The problem is, zombies come in swarms from all sides, and THEY. NEVER. STOP. They just keep coming, and soon you're holed up in some dingy janitor's closet down to your last two shells, and the zombies are moaning for your brains outside the door, scratching at the hinges. In no time, they're feasting on your sweet, succulent brain juices and licking their fingers.

Okay, they won't get you like that. (Sorry, that was graphic.) But the persistence thing is true. At first, zombies won't affect you, but after a while, all that whining and griping and pessimism coming from so many sources starts to wear you down and seep in. It's hard to tell why pessimism is so seductive, like jalapeño chips and Hawaiian pizza, but it is. It's like gravity, pulling you down.

Before you know it you are moaning and complaining just like the zombies. K-POW! You're infected! Even worse, now you'll start looking for happy people and laughing children to contaminate with your ugly stupid misery. If you're not careful, their apathy will crush your spirit and all their negative zombie-thoughts will gnaw at your brains.

Let's face it: No one wants anything gnawing on their brains. So, let's talk about . . .

// How to dominate zombies

It's easy: Shoot them in the head with a 12-gauge. Works every time.

Wait . . . sorry, no—that's the movies. In your quest for world domination, never shoot people. Ever! Shooting people is a blatant violation of Rule Number 2. No, in life, the best way to dominate a zombie is to simply refuse to stoop to their level.

There's something you need to understand, and it might hurt to hear, because everyone wants life to be easy and happy and hurt-free like skipping in the sunshine through a meadow full of posies and frolicking kittens. But here's the thing:

BAD THINGS ARE GOING TO HAPPEN TO YOU.

And not just you . . . everyone. No one is immune to pain and pitfalls. The problem with zombies is that they think they're the only ones who deal with hard times. So they go all "woe is me" and wander around passing out invitations to their selfish little pity parties. Zombies are, frankly, pathetic. They just don't get it. They don't realize one of the most important truths about dominating your world:

// It's not what happens to you, it's how you respond

A while back the Department of Homeland Security almost arrested me, in Kansas.

I was in the airport, fresh from a speaking engagement, in the herd of human cattle that pushes its way through every security checkpoint. After they ran my bag through the conveyor-belt machine, a guy on the other side wearing thin white gloves asked if he could do an additional screening on my bag.

No problem, I said. Screen away.

Besides, who was he kidding? What if I had said, "No! I think you've screened my bag enough!" I'm sure he wouldn't have said, "Sorry, Mr. Shipp. My fault, have a nice flight!"

I think not. I think special forces troops would have dropped out of the ceiling, pinned me to the floor, and rescreened my unmentionables anyway.

To avoid that kind of spectacle, I told him to go ahead and have his way with my bag. So he took it to a gray machine off to the side, got out this tweezer-looking thing, and used it to rub down my bag with a cloth that looked like an Oxy pad.

He stuck the cloth in a machine, the machine calculated, and then it went . . .

BEEP

Which was odd. Because the beep meant my bag had just tested positive for explosives.

The guy in the white gloves frowned, because bags are not supposed to beep. "You have anything in this bag we should know about?"

"Um . . . no?" I offered.

So he ran it through again.

BEEP

Which made him frown again and glance at me uncomfortably. Then he snatched up the intercom, rattled off some code phrase with a "niner" in it, and suddenly I was surrounded by ten Homeland Security agents in black pants and white shirts. They circled my bag as if ready to play a very serious game of ring-around-the-rosy.

The agents opened up my bag and looked through it, which was an awkward public spectacle because when I travel for speaking enagements I often bring props. (Not props like respect, but props like story aids.) First, they pulled out a string of fake leaves from a Crocodile Hunter bit I did back then. Then a black-and-white stuffed dog I used for the routine about talking to my pets. And, for the finale, in front of the whole airport security line, they pulled out my lifelike, bed-pillow-size SpongeBob SquarePants doll, which I mostly use for companionship. Don't judge.

Meanwhile they made me wait in this glass cubicle as if I were Hannibal Lecter. I remember an old lady walked by me, shook her head, and spat, "You're sick!"

It wasn't a good day.

Eventually, they figured out there wasn't a nuclear weapon in my carry-on and let me go.

"Have a nice flight," the white-gloved security officer said, as he gave me back my SpongeBob and my bag.

The ordeal could have stressed me out, 'cause I nearly missed my flight, but I chose to let it go. Finally, after that twenty-minute adventure, I got on the plane. There was just one seat left, and I knew it had to be mine. I settled in and glanced over at my seat partner, a squinting guy with a comb-over hairdo who was wearing a plaid, short-sleeved collared shirt and glasses.

"How are you?" I asked.

Keep in mind, airport security had just robbed my of my dignity and I was narrowly escaping Kansas with my freedom. I couldn't have expected the response this guy gave me. It was so thoroughly laced with profanity that I cannot repeat the actual words here. So I will still tell you what he said, but in place of the offending words, I will use the word "bunny." Ready? He said:

"I want you to rip off my <bunny> head. Just pull my <bunny> brains out of my <bunny> head, throw my <bunny> brains on the ground, and then reattach my <bunny> head to my <bunny> neck."

This sounded serious. I asked him if everything was OK. He said yeah, he just had a headache.

A headache? Please.

Now, this entire airport experience, from the intensive bag check to the guy with the dramatic headache, reminded me that in life it's not what happens that's most important, it's how you deal with it. It's your attitude.

Above all, your attitude is a choice. In fact, your attitude is one of the few things in your life that you have complete control over.

I could have very easily popped off at the guy on the airplane who was sitting there disrespecting bunnies for no reason. I could've said, "Oh yeah? You think you've had a bad day? I just spent the last twenty minutes . . ." But I chose not to. Why? Because it's pointless to compare stories of misfortune with zombies.

Now, it's not realistic when something horrible happens to stand up and yell, "That's wonderful!" But seeing a difficult situation and knowing that one day—maybe not that very moment, but in the future—you're going to find something positive in it, that's having an attitude that shows integrity.

Whenever a zombie faces hardship (and for a zombie, EVERY-THING is a hardship—zombies get bummed out when they get the *wrong kind* of pony for their birthday), they just give up. Usually, they've already given up inside.

Because of this, they don't really pose much of a threat if you stand up to them. They aren't out to get you. Zombies, like misery, love company. They're after attention. They're sad and lonely, and want you to feel sad and lonely with them (it's weird). If they swipe at you with their grimy corpse-arms and try to bring you down, it's just because they want you to see your world the same way they see theirs: Like a dung beetle rolling a ball of crap across the Sahara. If you make it clear you're not going to slip into their pattern of sad-sack malaise, zombies will do what they always do. They'll give up.

(They won't give up complaining, mind you. But they might stop complaining around you.)

Sometimes horrible, ugly, difficult things happen. Sometimes it hurts, and the last thing you want to do is be positive. But try. You might not be able to change the situation, but you can change your perspective. You might even learn something.

// How to rescue zombies

Some zombies just really need someone to talk to. Maybe they used to be a normal, happy-go-lucky alive person and then—*bam!*— suddenly they're the walking dead and they don't even know what happened. Maybe they just need to talk things out. The trick is re- directing the conversation away from the zombie's "problems" and toward other things. Here's the absolute BEST (zombies don't know what to do with this): Talk about what you're thankful for.

'Cause here's the thing: Optimism is also contagious. Grati- tude is also contagious. Like yawning, but better. Any time a zom- bie goes into Debbie Downer mode, look for ways to steer the conversation in a positive direction. That doesn't mean you should grin and giggle like an idiot, chattering on and on about lollipops and dolphins. Maybe it means reminding the zombie that things could be a lot worse. If a zombie complains about the bus being late, and how it's been raining for three days in a row, you could politely mention how fortunate the zombie is to not be an African orphan whose parents died from AIDS-related complications.

Or you can offer solutions. Let's say the zombie has been com- plaining about homework, about how obnoxious a teacher is. Ask the zombie questions, and turn it into a project that you and the zombie can work on to improve his life. Maybe he'll appreciate it, and maybe he'll start looking for solutions rather than pouting like a kid whose balloon just popped.

If you can't seem to snap zombies out of their funk, sometimes

the best thing to do is leave them alone, especially if they're starting to bring you down with their hopeless attitude. Sometimes
zombies are happy just to stagger about, gazing at their shoes,
moaning and droning. If that's the case, you're best off just getting
out of there.

Seriously, it's not worth it. If the zombie comes around to living the good life someday, you can be friends again. Until then,
you're not doing yourself (or them) any favors by following them
down the rabbit hole.

12.

Puppies

Yes, puppies. It's hard to turn down a puppy, or any baby animal for that matter. They're adorable as a ladybug's ear, and they look like they'll love you forever and ever.

But the truth is, puppies can be the devil. They chew through anything if given the time. They poop in shoes and on carpets and pretty much everywhere else you don't want them to poop. (So . . . yeah, pretty much on everything you love and cherish, including themselves.) They need walks and water and food. You can't leave them alone for too long, and you can't take a vacation without figuring out what to do with them. It's not that puppies are intentionally jerks, it's that they need a lot of attention and care. And—surprise!— they grow up into dogs . . . and caring for a dog takes a dump-truck load of responsibility.

No one ever thinks about that, though. They just see the innocent little puppy with its pleading eyes, and they take it home with them, not realizing the decades of commitment they just signed up for.

Puppy

Class—Puppy

Disguises—Supercute girlfriends; Pranks; Sex

Mission Statement—To get you to invest in them by appearing fun, then overwhelm you with consequences and responsibility

Signature Moves—Blindsiding you with hidden costs and consequences; Saddling you with responsibility; Taking up time; Crowding out dreams

How to Defeat Them—Think ahead

// Puppies aren't going to be the same for everyone

Puppies can be silly, like a nickname you pick for yourself when you're eleven that's going to be kind of embarrassing ten years down the road if it sticks. Or they can be serious, like pursuing a relationship to the point where you're talking about getting married before you've ever held down a steady job or even figured out who you are yet.

Here's the thing: In and of themselves . . .

// Puppies are innocent

They have zero ill will and are simply acting according to their true puppy selves. There is nothing wrong with puppies. Puppies are good things, like cupcakes and sunny days. However, puppies generally bring more than cuddly playfulness into your life. Puppies also guarantee long-term consequences.

And that's where they get you.

// Signature moves

Let's say you've got this girlfriend, and she's hotter than a thousand splendid suns, and you guys get along great. You guys are in love, and it's REAL love, and you want to get married. Only catch is . . . you're seventeen.

Sure, those feelings are real, but have you considered what you'll have to give up to be with her?

Listen carefully, 'cause I'm NOT telling you to be selfish here; I'm telling you to think ahead.

Do you have what it takes to meet this girl's needs? Will you have time for your friends, your hobbies, your band? Will you be able to handle a long-distance relationship if you pursue your perfect college? Will you pick a different college to stay closer together? Will that affect your long-term goals? Will you be spending more time on dates and less time on your dreams? Are you ready to commit to each other NOW and stay faithful for however many years it takes before you're actually ready to marry and spend your life together . . . and then keep at it for all the years after that?

Are you willing to make sacrifices? Accept consequences? Take responsibility?

Do you have an impending headache from all these tough questions?

Because if you do . . . it's time to pause for a sec. Try to look at the puppy objectively. It's not the puppy's fault, but puppies often sabotage your plan to dominate your world. You want to feel closer to your boyfriend, so you sleep with him . . . and get knocked up. Oops. Now you're a single teenage mother and THE REST OF YOUR LIFE IS DIFFERENT. Sorry, too late. You bought the puppy, so now you get to deal with the consequences.

Puppies usually have pure intentions. But if you rush in to

scoop up every adorable puppy you see without thinking about the implications ahead of time, you're going to have a lot of regrets.

So, betcha wanna know . . .

// How to dominate puppies

You know that squishy gray mass in your head? It's there for a reason. THINK. Think long and think hard. Dominating puppies—choosing the right puppies at the right time—is all about foresight. Looking ahead. Taking stock. Working it through.

Puppies will almost always dominate your world if you get involved on impulse or based purely on emotion. Ask yourself: "Am I ready for a dog?" If not, don't buy the puppy.

I grew up crazy poor. Not, like, flies-on-my-face poor. But poor.

Because of this, I think I made a decision early on that I'd never hurt for money when I grew up. I didn't want to put my future family through the stress and insecurity that can come from unstable finances. Noble, right?

Not really.

Money became my puppy. Now, there's nothing wrong with money. It's neutral. It's useful. But having it and managing it and spending it comes with a lot of responsibility. How you use it is what matters.

I thought to myself, "When I have $X,XXX.XX amount, I'll be happy and stable and secure."

Amount acquired.

"Well, that's nice," I thought, "but it's not enough. When I have $XXX,XXX.XX, *then* I'll be happy and stable and secure and a better person."

Done.

Why am I still freaked out? Because money doesn't make you happy. But everyone thinks it will. Including me.

Me? I was greedy. And irresponsible with money. In fact, my abuse of money got me thrown in jail once . . . but that's another story.

Dealing with puppies is all about you. If you're confident and strong, if you take the time to think about what you're getting into, you'll walk right by that pet store window without falling prey to the tug of desire. Being strong doesn't mean not *feeling* desire, it just means taking the time to step back and spend a few moments thinking about the consequences of what you're getting into. Simple as that.

// How to rescue puppies

Puppies are fine. Seriously. They aren't malicious villains or dangerous threats to society in and of themselves. You can let them be; they don't need "rescuing" from their puppy-dog ways. Puppies are only bad because, well . . . usually the timing is wrong. Or, you're not ready to handle the responsibility or the consequences of getting involved. Come back later, and you might find you are. But in the meantime, it's not going to do you or the puppy any good to cling to each other. Keep this in mind: The puppy you care so much about may be better off without you, too . . . at least for now. It might hurt, but you and the puppy will be better off for the time being.

Down the road, when you're more established and confident with where you're headed, it might be time for a puppy. Until then, pat it on the head, smile, and move on.

13.

STOP! Are YOU a Villain?

As you read through the last seven chapters, perhaps you felt a twinge of guilt. Or several twinges. Maybe you even had a full-fledged seizure. Perhaps you're starting to worry that you're not the hero of this story after all . . . but that you are actually a villain!

Maybe you wondered "Is that me? Am I a vampire sometimes?" or "OMG I'M A PUPPY." Maybe you read about pirates, set down the freshman you were stuffing into a garbage can, and thought, "Perhaps my life is fraught with such malevolent diversions as this. After some introspection, I solemnly vow to cease my belligerence."

Don't worry. We all make mistakes now and again. Like I said, there's a little villain in all of us, even the heroes. Some heroes have kind of shady pasts, to tell you the truth. I mean, before he became

Iron Man, Tony Stark was a Ruthless *arms dealer*, for crying out loud. Can anyone say "selfish pirate"?

What's important is to stop making the same mistakes.

// First step? Admit you've screwed up.

I'll go first: I've been a villain. And, yes, I'm the dude who's writing this anti-villain manifesto. Ironic, I know. Go ahead, call me a hypocrite. A failure. I admit it—I'm not always the hero I wish I was.

I'm gonna be honest with you. I've . . .

- flipped out on my best friend for things that weren't her fault
- ditched an ex-girlfriend at a concert because she was annoying me
- used my words to tear people down
- skipped out on a restaurant bill
- assassinated a neighbor's ostrich while playing home-run derby . . . and lied about it to protect myself (true story, btw)
- bullied other people to make myself feel better
- wished people well to their face . . . and secretly hoped they would fail
- talked bad about some people behind their backs
- made promises I CHOSE not to keep
- jumped through hoops to be on a TV show
- neglected to make time to take my godson fishing
- prioritized money over people's feelings
- tricked people into doing what I want

- sucked up to strangers to try to impress them, and been a jerk to people who actually know me
- been too proud to say thank-you—I didn't truly say thank-you to my foster parents until I was twenty

In other words, I've been a pirate, a zombie, a ninja, and a vampire. And I'm not proud of this stuff. I'd rather stop writing right now, hold down the Backspace key, and just delete the whole list. Pretend it never happened. Hold up the mind-zapper thingie from *Men in Black* and erase the whole shebang from my mental hard drive. But if you lie to yourself and pretend everything's peachy, you'll never change. You'll just gradually convince yourself that it's OK to be a villain. You'll start to believe your own propaganda.

By exposing these villainous things I've done, I hope it stops me from being a villain in the future.

So, here's a challenge for ya: Write out the crap you're not proud of. On paper. In pen. No erasing allowed.

Be honest with yourself. Admit the stuff you'd rather forget you'd ever done—the times you've operated like a villain and not like a hero. It won't be easy, and I know you'd rather not do it at all. It takes serious guts to look yourself in the eye and call things like you see 'em. But you need to get this stuff off your chest.

Admitting your mistakes is the first step toward moving on. All this villain stuff . . . it's not who you want to be. It's not who you are.

These things don't define you.

But remember what we talked about in Chapter 4: You wanna

be a hero, you've gotta play by the rules and stop trying to dominate other people's worlds.

And that's not all.

// Now you need to apologize

If you've been a villain at any point, it's not enough to admit that to yourself. It's time to face your victims, confess your dastardly deeds, and ask their forgiveness.

Yeah, I know. This prospect has about as much appeal as eating a garden slug. But the truth is, it's hugely important, no matter how big or small the offense. I don't care if you called them a name or savagely disemboweled their parakeet—EVERY villainous action causes injury and subtracts from other people's lives. You may not understand or realize how much you've hurt your victims.

If you've treated your girlfriend without respect, taken advantage of her, or cheated on her, your actions have taught her that she has no value. Needless to say, this is a serious, serious injury. If you don't try to make it right, she might start to believe the lie you've told her and spend the rest of her life thinking she deserves poor treatment. She might even expect the same behavior from her next boyfriend!

It's not enough to just stop. Let your victims know you were wrong. They will appreciate it and, hopefully, they'll forgive you. Even if they don't—even if they choose to be a zombie about it— you'll have done the right thing. 'Cause that's what heroes do.

Part 3

HOW to DOMINATE YOUR WORLD

14.

You and What Army?

Welcome to your world, fledgling hero.

Now that you know who the villains are (and have successfully confirmed that you're not one of them), you'll notice that your world is completely and utterly overrun by the bad guys. Villains call the shots; they run the show. They are sneaky, they are powerful, they are destructive and deceitful, and they are everywhere. They hold the vast majority of humans enslaved to their will. Ah, yes . . . your world is a hostile place, infested with villains and fraught with danger. So, here is your mission:

I do hereby charge you to go ye out into the scary outer darkness of the wide, wide world and slay the hoard of invincible ghosts, devious ninjas, merciless pirates, controlling robots, bloodthirsty vampires, brain-eating zombies,

and perilous little puppies by yourself using only your
bare hands and an herbal tea bag.

Godspeed! Live long and prosper . . .

. . . for, like, fifteen seconds.

Let's face it, you don't stand a chance against all those villains.
Not on your own. Not with a tea bag. So listen up, 'cause this is
good, sweet news:

// The whole world is NOT out to get you

It's not. Your world, although filled with villains in disguise, is also
home to a whole posse of people who will watch your back in a
pinch. You don't have to fight all your battles alone.

In fact, it's best if you don't try. Here's the thing: As a hero, you
don't have the right to dominate anyone else's world (see Rule
Number 2), but you CAN help them dominate their worlds . . .
and they can help you. Being a hero isn't just about NOT being a
villain or keeping out of people's way. Heroes are team players.

Allies, sidekicks, mentors, sensei, confidants, costars—call
them what you will—you can recognize your teammates by their
general goodwill. You'll find allies everywhere in various forms, but
they'll always have this in common: Selfless concern for others. Allies are fellow world dominators who've become so good at beating
back their own villains that they want to help you succeed, too.
They're heroes who want to help.

The truth is,

// You'll never make it on your own

Seriously. You need others to help you, to learn from and help you up when you stumble. And if you're one of those people with the agility of a mountain goat who almost never stumbles and who rarely makes mistakes, don't get cocky. (They say "pride goes before a fall" for a *reason,* you know.) Instead, help others along the way. They'll be thankful, you'll be a real hero, and you'll have someone to lean on when dark days eventually come. It also feels good.

In your life, no matter what your plan or goals, you're going to need others to help you get there. The "self-made man" is a myth. Bill Gates didn't build Microsoft on his own. Michael Jordan couldn't have beat the Lakers to win his first NBA championship by himself. Without others, Albert Einstein would've just been a really smart dude with awesome hair.

This whole idea of "you've gotta do it yourself" is complete and total garbage. Seriously, the very best way to learn to do anything or be anything is to get a mentor. A coach. Someone to encourage you. Someone who's been there, done that, and got the overpriced, slightly faded, two-sizes-too-big tourist T-shirt to prove it.

My life would seriously be lame without the mentors I've had.

I have a group of friends with whom I run forty miles a week. Yes, I am a beast/marathon runner. No more "husky" jeans for me. (Can't they think of something more dignified to call those?) When these folks took me out for a run the first time (and kicked my butt), I wanted nothing more than to find some friends my own age who slept in, played Nintendo all day, and ate Cheetos. Seriously, I do love Cheetos. (If only they came with a moist towelette.) But these guys have helped push me to be better.

The point isn't the miles we run, although it's fun (now that I've stopped wheezing). It's the hilarious, challenging, honest, direct, inspiring, random conversations we have when we're together. These guys and gals on Team Running Revolution have become some of my best friends. And each of them (yes, even you, Eric) have taught me something important about being a good friend; having a family, relationships, business; dealing with disappointment; and what 5 A.M. looks like.

My wife, Sarah, has taught me how to trust. My foster parents basically taught me everything I know, and I think one day I will owe them a kidney or something. Jamie Oliver has taught me about business and life balance. Frank Kern taught me about packaging my message in a way that actually gets people to listen. Kirk has been the big brother I never had. The guys at Dot&Cross saw the big picture way before I did.

Point is, you need a mentor. A coach. Maybe a posse. At the very least, you need to find someone doing what you want to do really well, or living how you want to live, who will teach you how to get there yourself.

So, how do you approach this person? Do you poke them on Facebook? No! Do you call them, e-mail them? "Hey, I'm some kid. What's up?"

Here's the lowdown:

STEP 1. People of awesomeness are busy. Don't waste their time. Go to them prepared, organized, and humble.

STEP 2. Reach out with a plan. Here's who I am; here's why I think you're awesome; I want to learn from you; and I have six specific questions I can e-mail you if you don't mind.

STEP 3. Continue to invest in that relationship. Offer to buy them coffee or lunch. It will be money well spent.

Treat your allies well. And don't just expect them to be there for you; be there for them, too.

Often, our allies provide more than help. As people, we actually NEED other people just to keep us from going crazy.

And now, a lesson from history:

By the time he was thirty years old in 1935, Howard Hughes was one of the richest and most famous men in the world. He built an empire producing big-budget films and dating hot actresses—picture a cross between Steven Spielberg and Brad Pitt—and was one of the megacelebrities of his time. He did what he wanted, even if it was risky or weird. When the whim struck him to fly planes and break airspeed records, he did it. When he wanted to fly around the world, he did it.

As time wore on, though, Hughes became reclusive and began to slip into mental illness. He became obsessed with the size of peas, and surrounded himself with boxes of Kleenex, which he would sort over and over again in stacks. He developed an addiction to painkillers, codeine, and morphine, and fell further into madness until he was living as a complete hermit. He ordered his servants not to look him in the eye, kept one film on a constant loop so that he watched it 150 times, and refused to cut his fingernails or hair except once a year.

Not a good way to end up.

Despite his wealth, his fame, his films, his aviation high jinks, and the girls he dated, Howard Hughes is remembered for being an insane recluse. Not exactly the legacy of a world-dominating hero. So, what's the takeaway here?

There's a famous saying: Live together . . . die alone.

If you're serious about dominating your world, you need to stay close with your friends so you don't end up going crazy and die a sad, bitter lonely old person.

If you try to go it alone, you do so at your own risk.

15.

How to Own Your
Own Identity

In the war for your world, your identity is the single biggest battle-ground. Take this hill and everything else will be much easier. Ignore this issue and, sooner or later, the villains will probably win. Trust me. I've seen this happen many times.

> **VILLAINY YOU'RE MOST LIKELY TO ENCOUNTER**
>
> GHOSTS; VAMPIRES; NINJAS

Why is this issue so important? Because . . .

// Your identity lies at the core of who you are

It has everything to do with who you believe you are and what you think you're capable of. It's the truth (or lie) that generates (or undermines) your self-confidence.

Your behavior will always follow your beliefs.

So if your mind is dominated by ghosts telling you you're worthless, hopeless, or not good enough . . . your very sense of self is totally WHIPPED. When you believe the lies, when you start accepting those labels as fact, you start to act like those lies and labels are true . . . and before you know it, you're sabotaging yourself. Suddenly, you've become easy prey for ninjas and vampires and pirates and zombies. They own you. And they're happy to help guide your life straight down the toilet.

OK, confession time:

// I shouldn't even be here

This topic of identity is very, very personal for me. Most of you guys know this (unless you skipped the "This Is Required Reading" section at the beginning of this book, in which case, I owe you a slap), but I had a pretty rough childhood, which led into my teenage years, which frankly were very, very miserable at times. You see, because of my past, growing up in foster care, the abuse, the neglect, the hurt that I experienced . . . I allowed that to label and define me. I allowed that to shape my identity and dictate who I thought I was going to be in the future.

I remember at one point this guy literally yelling at me: "Josh, you are just a punk, orphan, foster kid. That's all you're ever going to be. Nothing more. Nothing less." I mean, it was literally those words . . . I can still remember that guy saying them. And sadly, in that moment, I let those words label me. And I believed them. "Yeah, you know, I am a punk, orphan, foster kid. And I guess that's all I'm ever gonna be. Nothing more. Nothing less." It sank in . . . and I believed it.

And because I believed it, I acted out. I was the class clown. I was a rebel. I fought with my foster parents and got in trouble with the law. And I actually hated myself. There was a time in my life when I seriously thought about killing myself.

Fact: Fifty percent of foster kids end up in jail, dead, or homeless. And honestly, that is exactly where I was headed.

But then there was this moment . . . a moment that seemed unbelievably insignificant at the time. I was at one of my lowest points—this is when I was eighteen years old. I was dealing with depression big-time and felt completely worthless, so I tried to make myself feel better by spending tons of money I didn't have using bad checks. Things spiraled out of control fast and I ended up getting tossed in jail for a night. Very scary. But here's the thing: Oftentimes our moments of change are inspired by moments of absolute agony. No one changes until they face something hard, bump up against some resistance. You either get more set in your ways or are shaken up enough to say, "Screw it—this isn't working . . . I'll try something different." For me, I'd hit the bottom. And that was when my foster parents looked me in the eye, in their living room, and just simply said: "Josh, you are not a problem. You are an opportunity." And verily, verily I tell you, that little shift in perspective from a grown-up in my life forever shaped my identity.

The funny thing is, my foster parents had probably said that to me, like, a gazillion times before. I'll be honest—I would often tune them out. But at that moment, I was ready to hear it. I was ready to believe it.

I'm so thankful that they didn't stop telling me that. I'm so thankful that they didn't just write me off. Because everything I am today, everything that I have accomplished today, everything that I have done today, I can trace back to that one simple moment.

I should've ended up homeless; instead, I help change the world.

I'm living proof that changing your identity—changing your perception of yourself—changes EVERYTHING.

So let me ask you something . . .

// Who are you?

A simple question, just three little words. But it's also a question that is a lot harder to answer than it seems, particularly when we're young. Our identity is based on a mix of our personalities and our experiences, and the younger we are, the less our experiences have shaped us. You might feel like your personality shifts depending on where you are in life. That's OK—discovering who you are is a lifelong process. But the earlier you get started, the better off you'll be in the end. That saying about the early bird getting the worm? Yeah, that applies here. But with success and happiness instead of, you know, a worm.

Awesomeness Tip
If you don't figure out who you are, some villain will TELL you who you are. Don't let villains dominate your world!

There was this kid in my high school class everyone called "Stanky." I sat next to him in science class, so every once in a while I'd kind of sniff him. You know, take a deep breath through my nose to see how bad he smelled, because, I mean, you've gotta stink something awful to get the nickname "Stanky," right?

It was like scientific experiment for me, 'cause I'd write down on a scale of 1 to 10, with 10 being stinkiest, how bad he smelled.

Sniff sniff. 7.453
Sniff sniff. 8.162

You know what I discovered?

At the end of my experiment I discovered he smelled pretty good. Not bad. Like an 8. That's pretty impressive. I don't smell that good half the time.

You know what else I noticed? On his papers—in the upper right-hand corner—he would write that his name was "Stanky."

Kind of funny, right? At the time, I thought it was hilarious. But now I realize it's sad. 'Cause you see what happened? This dude let other people define him. Tell him who he was. Worst of all? It wasn't even true.

But that's how it works. If you don't figure out who you are, someone else will try to tell you who you are.

My fear? If you listen to them for long enough, if you let them label you for long enough, you just might start to believe it. You just might buy into it. You just might start writing that name on your paper.

Don't let your villains tell you who you are. That's lame. This is for YOU to decide. This is something you've gotta own for yourself.

It's hard, though, right? Gosh, I remember when I was in junior high and high school I had no clue who I was. I was kind of overweight, not very good in school, kind of a loner. But most people thought I was funny and I kind of liked that attention, so . . . it was all very confusing.

Maybe you know what I'm talking about. You may feel completely comfortable and outgoing with close friends. Maybe you're the joker everyone relies on for a laugh at your job, where your quick wit pours out clearer than natural springwater. But then at school you feel lonely and shy, and no one gets your sense of humor. It may seem weird, but trust me, it's a classic situation.

Everyone feels this way to some extent. Some people thrive under pressure and in new situations, and others work best when they know the boundaries and the people they're around. We all have places and situations where the solutions come more easily, where we're particularly capable.

The trick is figuring all this out. Here are some basic questions to get you started on your journey of self-discovery.

// First, what makes you unique?

You know those quizzes that people are always sending around on Facebook? Asking random, seemingly pointless questions like, "If you were a can of soup, what flavor would you be?" or "If you were an organic field, what crop would you grow?" They're kind of a waste of time, but they can also be strangely thought-provoking. Generally, the point is to get to know yourself and your friends a little better. And here's the thing about answering questions like that: You realize you're different from everybody else. OK, maybe someone else also picked Campbell's Chunky vegetable beef stew, too, but they probably did it for different reasons.

Everything from your favorite color to your favorite Disney princess says something about what makes you unique.

You know how your one friend always sneezes fifteen times in a row, and how that one guy in history class twirls his pen through his fingers when he's bored? Those are called quirks, and they're part of what makes different people different. See also: Habits, patterns.

Sometimes these things are harmless and fun. Sometimes they're embarrassing. Other times they're downright difficult to deal with . . . like picking up on the fact that you've only dated jerks, or that you tend to freak out when things don't go exactly according to plan, or that you have a habit of choking under pressure.

Still, detecting and examining these patterns is crucial. Usually, bad habits indicate that there's a ghost or a vampire or a ninja calling the shots somewhere. But until you recognize the pattern and address the cause, you'll be doomed to repeat the cycle forever and ever.

And now, a quick warning about vampires.

Sometimes being different or unique isn't always seen as a good thing, right? I mean, no one wants to be the weird one or the odd man out. But sometimes we're so scared of rejection (because of ghosts) that we feel the need to "fit in" by imitating or impersonating other people. Like this: You think so-and-so's cool and he thinks you're cool if you act like him, so you do act like him and feel a sense of belonging and identity . . . but get this—that's not your real identity. That's like turning into a robot that says the right things and does the right things just so you can be accepted by a vampire. LAME!

Look, there's nothing wrong with having role models. But just because your friends like a certain band or a clothing brand or a movie doesn't mean you have to! If you have to be like your friends just to be accepted by them, they're vampires . . . and they're probably not as cool as you think they are.

// Second, what do you love?

What makes you happy or gets you excited? You know those times when you just want to jump up and down and punch the air and maybe shout something like "WOOHOO!"

Pay attention to those things, activities, and situations, 'cause these are the things you love. Some of that may change over time, but a lot of it won't, so take notes. Make a list of things that make you absolutely ecstatic. Same thing goes for the stuff you don't like—the stuff that annoys you and bums you out and makes you want to rend your garments and throw feces like an angry chimpanzee. Make a list of all that stuff, too. Some of the bad stuff (like homework or eating vegetables, you baby) you'll just need to get over (don't become a zombie!). But pay close attention to the rest of the stuff, because if you can figure out what you love and build your life around it—while avoiding the things that give you heartache—your happiness will be genuinely limitless.

// Third, what are you good at?

It's important to recognize when you feel strong and when you don't. When you're asked to lead a group, do you roll into the fetal position, or do you stand tall and take charge? When you're asked to write an essay on a book you like, do you poke aimlessly at the keys and hope no one actually reads it or do you blow through it like the Olympic gold-medal sprinter Usain Bolt?

Whether you believe it or not, there is something about you that sets you apart. You are good at something. You may not be the absolute BEST in the world at this thing, but you're miles ahead of most people.

Think about your friends and your family. What makes you different from them? What skills do you have they don't?

One way to figure it out is to ask them. Your parents and friends might have a perspective on your talents you can't see, so just ask 'em straight up. You're likely to get a whole stack of compliments in return.

Remember though, you're your own person. Maybe your mom thinks you're the best laundry folder in the world, but that doesn't mean you want to spend your life folding clothes. So, take other people's assessments of your talents with a shaker-full of sea salt. One of Einstein's grade-school teachers said he'd never amount to much and people wrote me off as a lost cause when it came to communicating.

Who's laughing now?

In the end, you're the best judge of what makes you feel strong, capable, and fulfilled. Pursue those things. The things that frustrate you and make you feel stupid and start to cry a little? Push through them when you have no other choice (for me, this was math in school), but if you're given the opportunity (say, in college or in your career), leave the stuff you're bad at for the people who love it and rock at it and stick with your strengths.

// What do you stand for?

Let me ask you this: If you had a million dollars and you had to give it away, what organization or cause would you give it to? Is there anything in the world today that makes you so sad and angry that you want to change it?

I think all of us have something to say to the world. Something that no one else can say the same way.

This won't necessarily be a speech or a book or a great work of art. It could be anything. It could be a kind heart or a knack for fixing cars or the ability to lead others or a sense of justice and honesty. The point is, you have *something* to give back.

The problem is, the vast majority of the world never learns this. They live regular old boring lives until, at the end of their lives, they die.

I'm not saying you need to be a politician or an Olympic athlete or an arena rock star. I'm saying you have to be YOU, and part of being you—part of being a world-dominating hero—is using what makes you unique and what you love and what you're good at to make a difference, to communicate a message however you're gifted, wherever you are. If you live the best story you can live, it's bound to inspire someone else.

That's the bottom line here. That's what the goal of owning your own identity really is. It's about reaching the point where we know what we want to say, and we spend our lives saying it. Standing for something and working for something greater than ourselves. Sure, we'll probably stumble and fall all along the way, but we won't give up.

I won't lie . . . I'm sure money and power and fame are great and all. You can help people with money and power. You can get your message across with fame.

But in the end, they're not all that important or even that impressive. What you want to do and what you want to say has to be bigger than those things.

Here's a story:

David Johnson was born in Cleveland, Ohio. He was the third of three children, with two older brothers and a younger sister. His family was poor. When David was two years old, his father went out to pick up pizza for the family's dinner, but he never came back.

After that, things were harder. David's mom worked full-time at Walgreens during the day, and picked up extra shifts at a Mexican restaurant in the evenings. David and his brothers were forced to take care of themselves, and David watched as they began selling weed to help out. When they got good at that, they moved on to selling crack and heroin. David's oldest brother was shot and killed during a drug bust, and his other brother became an addict.

David promised his mother he'd do better. He avoided the quick cash of drug-dealing. He found a pastor in the neighborhood who counseled him, and he worked hard in school. His teachers saw his potential, that he was uncommonly good with numbers, and a hard worker.

Still, college was out of the question. His mother made just enough money for rent and food, and David had no idea about how to go about applying.

But David's economics teacher felt he could make something of himself. She helped him apply not only to college, but for scholarships suited for boys with his background. He was accepted at the University of Michigan. The scholarships helped, but they weren't enough, so David worked full-time while he was in school at Ann Arbor, all four years.

And despite all that, David graduated seventh in his class, with a degree in business.

Then he got hired at a Fortune 500 company. He worked his way into management, then upper management, then all the way

up to become the company's chief financial officer (that's a big deal
in the business world, FYI).

He made millions and millions of dollars. He had fourteen cars
and silverware made of gold. He had engineers build him a house
that could float in midair.

THE END.

Based on that story, here's what we know about David: He accomplished more than anyone could imagine, he lived an incredible
story, and then, when he reached the top, it stopped.

Here's another end to David's story:

He made millions and millions of dollars. He moved back to the
neighborhood where he grew up and bought a modest house where
he lived with his wife and children. He spoke to his old friend,
the pastor, and together they started a foundation for kids growing up without fathers. He lent money to local businesses in the
neighborhood. The first business was a bakery, then a barbecue
joint, then an old-fashioned barbershop. The economy in David's
neighborhood boomed. He added on to his modest house, building
a giant dining room and a first-rate kitchen. Four nights per week,
David would have people from the neighborhood over for dinner,
which he and his family prepared themselves. David's dinner parties
had all sorts of guests—kids from David's foundation, Cleveland
politicians, the bakery owner—all together at the same table, eating
good food and laughing at great stories.

Which story is better? Sure, the second story didn't have a
levitating house, but who really cares about a levitating house?

No one would've faulted David for never going back to Cleveland. He could've lived in Paris or New York. In fact, that's what we expect of people who become enormously wealthy.

But David knew who he was. He knew where he came from, and how he'd been raised. He knew there were thousands of boys just like him who wouldn't get the breaks he had, and who would end up like his brothers. POOR BOY MAKES IT OUT OF INNER-CITY CLEVELAND, BECOMES WEALTHY BUSINESSMAN is a decent headline, but David wanted an even better one. Simply put, he didn't want to be the only one who "made it out."

So, who are you? And what are you going to do about it? How will who you are make the world a better place? If you don't believe you've got what it takes, you're listening to ghosts. Kick them in the mouth. Take it from me: Your story is an epic win waiting to happen.

WORLD DOMINATION CHALLENGE

In the back of this book, there's a short bio about me. It's one of those things publishers make authors do. It basically describes who I am in a few sentences. It's a little spare on the details, but it hits most of the essentials. Read it to get a feel for how this sort of thing works, then take a stab at writing your own. You can make it as long as you want, but five sentences is a good target.

16.

How to Deal with Your Parents

Ah, parents. Like it or not, your parents are a big part of your world. I'm sorry, but you don't have a choice in the matter. Those two misfits brought you into this world without even asking your permission and now you're stuck under their care.

Sure, they were probably there when your bloody little head burst forth into the world for the first time. Sure, they dutifully wiped and powdered your bottom every time you pooped until you were two years old (longer, for some of you; you know who you are). Sure, they burped and bathed you. Sure, they paid for your food and shelter and clothes. Sure, they generously donated half their genetic code to you.

For some reason, after all this, they act like you *owe* them.

I mean, c'mon! They *chose* to bring you into the world! What did they expect? That your diapers would just change themselves?

That you'd go hunt and gather and prepare yourself a balanced meal? Seriously, changing diapers and feeding and bathing and clothing—it's all part of the package; that's just what happens when you have a kid!

(In case you're slow, I'm employing a little something called sarcasm right now.) Let's face it . . . your parents *did* put in a lot of work. Sure, sometimes having them tell you "because I said so" is a little irritating, but . . . *meh,* showing a little respect couldn't hurt. Even when they screw up.

Oh, they DO screw up sometimes. But you knew that, right?

VILLAINY YOU'RE MOST LIKELY TO ENCOUNTER
GHOSTS; ROBOTS; ZOMBIES

Right about the time we reach sixth grade or so is when we start realizing our parents aren't perfect. After that, it's dicey for a while. Let's face it, our parents aren't always easy to live with. Sure, some parents are fairly awesome, but no one is perfect. Shoot, my biological parents didn't even stick around five minutes after I was born; they just packed up and left me crying in the hospital. I mean, you think you have it bad—I had twelve different sets of foster parents to deal with growing up. *Twelve.* Think about it. I'm not trying to be a zombie here, I'm just trying to give you some perspective. I've got lots and lots of experience in the whole dealing-with-parents category.

Parents have more impact in shaping our personality and choices than any other outside source, which is honestly kind of frightening, since we can't choose them. Even worse (and we may not want to admit this), but we're probably more similar to our parents than we think.

Our families can become a breeding ground for our loudest and most destructive ghosts, telling us where we'll fall short, and why we shouldn't even try.

"You're just like them," the ghosts whisper, pointing at your parents.

Not me, you're saying. *I'm nothing like my parents.*

Don't get me wrong, the ghosts are lying; you *are* different. But you'd be surprised by the family resemblance. Knowing those ghosts and knowing those similarities can help you break free.

// The pains of parenting

Let's return to one of my basic Josh-isms: *Seek to understand before you seek to be understood.*

This is a crucial knowledge biscuit, and I'll tell you why.

I became a parent recently, so I feel like I've got some insight into how this works. Admittedly, my son is tiny, so I haven't had to deal with neck tattoos, concealed weaponry, or learner's permits yet. Still, when you become a parent, you suddenly seem to gain some sliver of insight into why your parents act the way they do. And some of it is surprising.

First, your parents want the best for you. I mean it; they love you in a way you can't know until you have your own children. I'm telling you, it never made sense until I was in their position. All of a sudden, there was this pipsqueak creature living inside my wife, swimming around her belly and punching the edges. I could feel him in there. Sometimes I'd tap and I'd feel a tap back.

The tiny creature continued to get bigger until I could feel his back and his feet, and his hiccups.

And then, months later, London Alexander was born. He came into the world screaming, just like his dad. He was this little ball of skin and uncoordinated muscle, wiggling all over. He turned toward my wife and me when we spoke, and he knew, even then, that we were his parents.

When my wife was pregnant, I'd think about how great it would be to be a dad. I'd think about how my son would admire me, and how I'd teach him how to do manly things like box and talk back to authority figures (except me, of course). I read all these books talking about how important a father is in a son's life, how a boy looks up to his father like he was Batman.

The books were inspiring at first, but then I started to think about the prospect of my son becoming older. I thought about how there were all these mistakes that I knew I would inevitably make, and I worried that maybe every mistake I made would irreparably mess him up somehow, like if I fed him pureed peas rather than carrots, he'd end up being a guard at a maximum-security women's prison rather than a state senator.

Maybe the thing that broke my heart most was picturing him as a teenager. I know he'll be a better teenager than I was, but if he's even 1/100th as bad, I'm in for an ocean of hurt.

I think every parent wants the best for their children. They love their children with that same unexplainable love. They want their children to be healthy and happy, to follow their dreams and be successful and good. They want their child to love and respect them back, and they want to help their children become all they want to be.

If you're honest, most of you will realize you have a lot—or something, at least—to be thankful for. I've never met my own biological parents, but I owe my foster family my life. They were patient with me when everything was falling apart and they loved me enough to help me turn things around. We all need a grown-up or two who believes in us and sees our potential. Who looks past our screwups and mistakes and sees us for who we COULD BE: A hero . . . possibly in a cape of some sort. For the record, mine would be magenta, simply because I like the word. I don't even know what color that is.

// The perfect parent does not exist

There's a flip side, though.

In sitcoms, a parent makes mistakes, but the episode always ends with a lesson learned, and a wise word, as if every problem life throws at us can be solved in thirty minutes, or during a commercial break.

No parent understands fully how to bring this about. Before you were born, your parents were human. They were impatient and brash and unwise. They were quick-tempered and selfish. They made lots of mistakes, just like you.

After you were born, they were still those same two selfish

people. It's just that now they had this vast, cosmic quantity of love for you, often with very little grasp of how to let that out, how to really help you.

Every parent learns over time, but it's hard work. Harder than bench-pressing a cow or eating twenty chili dogs in five minutes. It means learning from a whole lot of mistakes, and going through a whole lot of pain and conflict.

Pain and conflict are a part of life. I know my son will confront ordeals I won't ever understand, but I'll tell you this: I do not want him to make the same mistakes I did. I would give my life if it meant he could avoid the situations I faced.

Chances are, your parents think the same way. It's sort of a universal parent feeling.

Just knowing this fact will help you and your relationship with your parents. If you treat your parents as villains, your life until you leave home (and probably a good chunk of your life after you leave home) will be miserable. It'll be a constant war of curfews and groundings and screaming matches.

If you can see your parents' perspective, though, and treat them as allies, you're gaining the best support you will ever have.

Now, seeing your parents' perspective doesn't necessarily mean it'll make sense. In fact, their perspective may be absolutely insane. I got a letter once from a girl who'd just received her learner's permit. Her dad was taking her out driving, but he wouldn't let her put her foot on the gas, and he told her to do a U-turn where there wasn't enough space. He wouldn't let her drive more than 20 miles per hour in a 30 mph zone.

"Apparently, my dad and the state of New York don't agree on what 'right' and 'wrong' driving is," she said.

I told her, as I'm telling you now, to look at his side of the story. It was possible her dad had been in a horrific car accident and had a hard time trusting others behind the wheel. Or maybe he was scared to go over 20 miles per hour, because he saw the movie *Speed* when he was in high school and it permanently scarred him.

(That's an old reference, so I'll explain. Keanu Reeves is trapped on a bus that's rigged to blow up if it goes under 40 miles per hour, so they can't stop, right? The bus ends up jumping a ninety-foot gap in a bridge, which would've been physically impossible. Still, it's a pretty good movie, and stars a young Sandra Bullock in her break-out role!)

Hey, I didn't say her dad's fears were rational. Most fears aren't.

More likely, her father was anxious. Learning to drive is a big moment in someone's life, and the girl's father might've been re-membering back to that moment I was telling you about, when he held his daughter for the first time, and now she's guiding a ton of metal down a narrow strip of pavement, with even larger chunks of moving steel flying by in the other direction.

By understanding her dad's perspective, the girl can commu-nicate better. If she recognizes how he feels and how big this mo-ment is for both of them, it's more likely than not that he'll ease up. If he was in a major car accident when he was younger, the girl could tell him she never wants to make that mistake, and would he please teach her how to drive well rather than coasting across a parking lot?

If the reason ended up being because of the movie *Speed,* then maybe a nice, quiet drive to the nearest asylum is in order. Just saying.

// Help them help you

There's only one proven way to deal with your parents, and it's through communication. That doesn't mean telling your parents every single detail of what's going on in your life (yeesh), but on the other hand, doing the opposite will make things WAY more difficult than necessary.

Case in point: I want my son to have a better life than I did, to avoid the same mistakes and to evade the horrible situations I was put in.

However, my son needs to face conflict to become a great man. If I shield him from everything, he will never learn to scale the obstacles in his way, because he'll be used to me bailing him out. Sometimes our parents need to be reminded of this, that life is hard, and that occasionally we need to make it on our own.

At the very least, you need to be honest with your goals. Tell your parents your goals. Tell them who you want to be, then ask if they can help get you there.

Basically, there are two options.

Option 1: Communicate honestly with your parents. Respect them, while simultaneously understanding they will not always be right, and they can operate only on what you've told them.

Outcome: Your parents become your most valuable ally. Their default mode is wanting the best for you. They want you to avoid the mistakes they made. They want you to succeed and be happy. Communicating well helps them understand how to best show their love and support for you.

Option 2: Lie to your parents about where you are and who you are with. Disregard their wishes. Roll your eyes whenever they get all up in your business.

Outcome: Since your parents control the keys to the house and car, and since they also have most of the money, they quickly become your most dangerous enemy. Constant fighting with your parents makes your life a nightmare. Soon, they don't trust you to make any of your own decisions. Eventually, you are finally honest with them, tearfully admitting your affair with a twenty-eight-year-old 7-Eleven cashier on a particularly touching episode of *Dr. Phil.* They send you to one of those camps for troubled kids in Utah, where borderline-psychotic former marines yell at you to make your bed.

It doesn't take Sherlock Homes (or even Harriet the Spy) to deduce which option is more beneficial for everyone. Up to you, though.

// One day it'll matter

I'm sorry to get all morbid and sad on you here, but recently I learned a close friend's father had died of a heart attack.

I encountered the man only twice, but each time it felt like I was meeting one of my oldest friends. He was one of those guys . . . one of those people who, when everyone gets up and says nice things at his funeral, every word is true. He led youth camps and mentored kids without fathers. I barely knew the guy, and yet I felt like he would dismantle a mountain stone by stone if I needed him to.

And now he's gone. Way too early, if you ask me.

My friend's dad was fortunate. Even though he's one of the most humble people I've met, I think he knew how much he meant to so many, and how much he meant to his daughters.

That's not always the case, you know. I don't know what it is in us that keeps us from telling people how much we love them and how much they mean. What I do know is we always have regrets when we lose someone we love. There's always something we wish we'd said, or a relationship we wish we'd mended.

I say all this because, let's face it, you'll have conflict with your family. That's a fact. Your parents will drive you crazy or let you down. My hope for you is that you don't let that stuff fester too long, or tear you apart and make you bitter and angry.

For me . . . I never even met my parents. And, I'll be honest, it's taken a lot for me to try to forgive them and move on. I could sit and finish the sentence "I wish . . ." all day long. Maybe some of you are in the same situation. You never met your dad, or your mom left or died when you were young. That's hard. But don't let what you've lost keep from you loving what you've got.

17.

How to Choose
Good Friends
(and Avoid Bad Ones)

The self-made individual is one of the pillars of American culture. Here in the United States, we've been taught to be self-reliant, tough. We've been taught we can be anything we want to be, on our own, if we just tug on our bootstraps hard enough from sea to shining sea. This land is your land, this land is my land . . . something like that. We are a nation, we've been told, of individuals, doing individual things, for individual gain.

It's all a lie.

Okay, it's not all a lie. Not the "be anything we want to be" part. That's true.

It's the individual part that's a lie. The truth is, no one makes it alone. Bill Gates, LeBron James, Barack Obama, the guys who invented Google . . . no one achieves anything without help. Especially the Google guys. I mean, there were two of them.

To dominate their worlds, each of those people needed a countless number of friends, from people their own age to mentors showing them the way. (We call them "allies," remember? Don't leave home without 'em.)

We are all products of our surroundings, of our upbringing and our family and our relationships and the cities or towns where we were raised. We are shaped by everything around us. But this does not mean we all become the same shape.

Besides your family and faith, no one will shape you more than your friends. Whether it's your best friend since you were seven years old, or a new acquaintance who shares your love of *The Simpsons,* our friends help frame how we see the world. We need friends for companionship, for sure, but we also need them to help us achieve our goals. If our friends raise hell, we're likely to raise hell.

Awesomeness Tip
Your Friends = Your Future.
Pick 'em wisely.

If our friends sit quietly and watch Disney movies on Friday nights, we're likely to do the same. If a friend is honest with you, you can more easily learn from your mistakes.

And since you can't choose your family, choosing your friends is one of the most important choices you'll make in your life.

No pressure.

// You gotta start somewhere

The first rule to having friends is, of course, making friends. Hey, don't look at me . . . I don't make the rules.

If you think about it, making friends seems like a ridiculously long and daunting process. Think about it: Do you remember how you met your closest friends? Do you remember every detail? Do you remember when you crossed the murky threshold from "acquaintance" to "buddy" to "friend"?

'Course not. These aren't the kinds of things that are marked by signposts. The memories I have of my best friends are all snippets: A conversation here, a bonding experience there . . . many, many years of talking about all sorts of subjects. It was never one single thing.

That's one of the nice things about friends. It's never one event. I saw an interview with Paul McCartney talking about John Lennon. Paul was fifteen and John was seventeen when they met, and Paul remembered he didn't like John.

"He smelled of beer," he said, and wrinkled his British nose in distaste.

Of course, if they'd left it there—if that was the one point they remembered—John and Paul never would've formed the most famous band in rock-and-roll history, the Beatles.

Making friends requires—and this is going to stun you—other people. You can find other people all sorts of places. Here are some places you might want to look for friends:

- Your classes at school
- Your sports team
- Your neighborhood
- Clubs or other organizations you're interested in
- Camp
- Church or synagogue or mosque or temple

Here are some places you probably shouldn't look for friends:

- Jail/prison/juvy
- During a bank robbery (particularly if it's the bank robber)
- Meth clinics
- Terrorist training camp

Now that you know who the villains are, try not to befriend them.

MOST COMMON FORMS OF VILLAINY IN FRIENDSHIP
NINJAS; GHOSTS; ZOMBIES; VAMPIRES; PUPPIES

The key to making friends is being approachable. If you join a club, for instance, and proceed to sit in the corner with your arms crossed and a brutal thousand-yard stare on your face, you're unlikely to be approached. If you're actively flipping people off, that tends to keep people away, too. You don't need to sit there like a panting golden retriever, but you should be willing to smile politely and make eye contact. (You'll hear a lot more about eye contact in this book. It's hard to explain why it's important, but it is.) Introduce yourself to others by saying "hey" and shaking their hand. Maybe even toss out a courteous little "nice to meet you."

If you do nothing else, *pay attention to the person's name.* In his book *How to Win Friends and Influence People,* Dale Carnegie points out that a person's name to that person is "the sweetest and most important sound in any language." I'm awful at remembering names, but there are a couple of tricks to remembering.

The first trick is to repeat the name back:

Me: *Hi, my name is Josh.*
Unnamed person: *My name is Gary Manilow.*
Me (trying not to laugh): *Gary. Nice to meet you, Gary.*

The second trick is name association. The name above would be easy to remember anyway, especially if you are into soft rock ballads from the 1970s and fluffy hair. Others are harder. When you hear the name, what does it remind you of? The more vivid the reminder, the better. Here's an example: Two neighbors moved in next door to our house. The husband's name was Landon, and the wife was named Carrie.

To me, Landon sounded vaguely like Lando Calrissian, the devious backstabber from Cloud City in the *Star Wars* movies (sorry for the continued references to *Star Wars,* but it's a movie almost everyone has seen and, let's be honest, it's awesome). Carrie Fisher was the actress who played Princess Leia. So, even when I forgot their name the next time I saw them, I still remembered *Star Wars,* and I was able to figure it out from there. Just as long as I didn't refer to them as Jabba the Hutt and Chewbacca, I was fine. See, it pays to have strategies.

// How are *you* doing?

OK, so you have the name part down. Now it's time to ask questions.

It's nice when someone wants to know about you, so a series of questions asked with genuine interest can prompt a conversation. I usually start by asking where someone is from (or what school they go to or what line of work they're in), which is a good first question because it opens up a series of follow-ups. At that point, it's time to listen. Pay close attention to answers, because that's where you'll find your next question.

> **Me:** *Where do you go to school?*
> **Gary Manilow:** *Leland High.*
> **Me:** *Oh, I go to Westmont. I think we just played you guys in soccer. Are you involved in any sports?*
> **Gary:** *No, I'm more of an artist myself.*
> **Me:** *Cool! What kinds of art?*

There you go—you've started a conversation. Maybe you find out he's a musician or a photographer or a writer or an actor. If you're into any of that stuff, you could talk about that. If you're not, keep asking questions: What do you do for fun? Are you planning on going to college? What you want to do with your life?

The point is, asking questions opens up opportunities for more questions until you've found common ground. Eventually, you're likely find a topic you're both passionate about, and the conversation will take off from there. At some point, the other person will probably start asking you questions, but don't be so eager to talk about yourself. Listening is one of the most valuable traits you can have in a friendship. Remember: Seek to understand before being understood.

There's another advantage to listening: People love to talk, and they love others to listen. If someone knows you listen to them, they'll love you for it. Sometimes you don't even have to do anything else but sit there and nod your head. When you're a good listener, people will go to the ends of the earth for you. It's odd but true. Listening might be your most valuable secret weapon. And anyone can do it.

// Finding friends in odd places

Of course, there are times when you just don't click. That happens. Maybe you don't have much in common with the other person. I've found, though, that some of the closest friendships happen with people we never thought we'd get along with. It's like that saying: "Opposites attract."

After a few good conversations—or even one—you can keep in contact. With social networking, you can find the person on Facebook or MySpace, particularly if they're a friend of a friend. Score one point for technology.

My friend Jordan was in the army, and he often talks about the close bonds he built with his fellow soldiers. The people he was stuck with were from all different backgrounds, with all different interests. When we choose our friends, we often pick people who are similar to us, but it was hard for Jordan to find people just like him in the army, so his best friends were a hospital administrator from Maryland, a computer nerd from rural Oregon, and an engineer from Indiana. Most of the time, they didn't like the same movies or music, but they found common ground in a common mission and in common circumstances.

You'll never guess how I met my best friend. I've known this guy since I was five, longer than anybody else in my life. How did we meet? Well, I was in a gang in kindergarten (I told ya I was a gangsta) and he beat me up and rubbed my face in the grass . . . which activated my asthma . . . and I went to the hospital.

This was our first interaction.

Now we're best friends. Go figure.

I'm not suggesting you beat someone up and activate their asthma and then ask 'em to hang out. I'm saying sometimes we find friends when we least expect it.

We can see a movie with anyone, really. We can laugh with strangers. But friends are there for moments that are tough and challenging. That's space you let few people into. And that's what friends are for.

You might meet those sorts of friends at your work or in school, but the friends we least expect to make can end up being our closest allies. Funny how that works out.

And now, a word from your mother:

// Don't take candy from strangers

Knowing how to meet people and strike up a conversation is all well and good, but you shouldn't just make friends with anyone who'll have you.

The kindly man offering you a Butterfinger and a ride home in his unmarked van probably doesn't own a candy shop. And that group that gets together on Tuesday nights to spray paint profane words on public buildings probably isn't role-model material.

A lot of people who seem friendly and accepting at first eventually turn out to be villains. Remember, villains don't often announce themselves and their evil intentions. Even pirates know how to turn up the charm to disarm a careless sucker looking for a friend or somewhere to belong. But they don't really care about you; they care about what they can *get* from you. They'll win you over . . . then slit your throat and pick your pockets. Ninjas are the same way. Puppies will distract you and take up all your time, zombies will bring you down, and vampires—alluring as they are—will drain you of your identity and enslave you.

Villains love the insecure. Insecure people are desperate for friends and generally fall in with the proverbial wrong crowd before they know what's happened.

Worried this might be you? Turn around and face your ghosts. The lies you've believed that make you feel inferior or unlovable or unwanted or like somehow you deserve to be taken advantage of—these lies need to be taken outside, beaten, and replaced with the truth about you:

You are a hero. You have a story to tell. And NO ONE has the right to dominate your world.

Which brings me to a phrase you may have heard me say before:

// Your friends = your future

Want to see the kind of person you'll become over the next few years? Then take a good hard look at your friends. If they're serious about dominating their worlds and reaching their goals, they're going to help you do the same. If they're dropping out of school to deal drugs or overindulging on Cheetos, it's gonna rub off on you (the bad habits and the sticky orange stuff). Like it or not, your friends have a huge influence on you.

Not too long ago, MTV calls me up and invites me to be a coach on an episode of *MADE*. Originally I said "no"—they wanted to film in December and January, and I always take off those months and hang out at my house. And surf. And watch lots of cartoons and late-night infomercials about kitchen knives. Important stuff.

Then they told me about the girl I'd be coaching:

"Her name is Dominique. She's a foster kid like you. She had a wonderful relationship with her foster mom. And this year her foster mom died. Since then she's been in a downward spiral of bad behavior. She's been kicked out of her school several times, kicked out of juvy several times, and gets drunk a lot and gets into fights. She's a really cool kid who just needs someone to help her turn her life around."

"Dang you! Why'd you have to pull the foster kid card on me? Alright, fine, I'll do it. Where does she live?"

"Pittsburgh."

Crap. It's cold there in December. But I want to do it. I want to try to help this girl.

I'm stoked. I pack up. I fly out. I get to the hotel . . . and I get a text message from the producer: "Don't unpack . . . bad news."

He called me to give me the details. Dominique got out of juvy a day early on good behavior. But her friends took her out, got her drunk, and got her in a fight. And just like that, she was back in juvy for another month. We couldn't film the episode. She threw away her opportunity.

I was so bummed/sad/frustrated/concerned.

How the CRAP could her supposed friends take her out and get her drunk the night she gets out of juvy? Really? Really? I mean really? You *really* thought that was a good idea?

And therein lies the issue. So many of us wanna change things about ourselves, but what we are currently doing is just plain easier. It's more comfortable to stay in a rut. We know what to expect. It takes less effort.

Sometimes when we are trying to better ourselves, we have to distance ourselves from our old friends, old habits, old patterns. It's ignorant to think we can stand up to their peer pressure when time and time again we've proven to ourselves that we can't.

If your friends aren't helping you, and you're not really helping them . . . what are you doing? Just messing around? Holding each other back?

Dominique was one step away from turning her life around and choosing to dominate her world . . . and she threw that chance away because of her pirate/ninja frenemies. They blew it for her. And she let them.

Don't let that happen to you.

// Best friends 4-eva!

As you get to know someone, it's important to watch that person's character, and to treat your new friend the way you'd want to be treated (follow Rule Number 2). Be reliable and loyal. Stick with your friends even if they let you down on occasion—everybody stumbles now and then. Show grace and forgiveness. Be trustworthy and honest.

And, here's the kicker: You should expect the same things. If you open up about your shortcomings, your friends will appreciate your honesty and the fact you trust them. Friendships develop at all speeds, so don't rush things. Some people are more quiet and introspective than others, and can take a while to open up.

There's more to character than determining if someone is a "good friend." Like I said before, your friends become one of your most important choices. A good friend can become your most powerful ally, and a bad friend can take you down all kinds of dangerous roads. It's harder to say "no" to our friends than to strangers, especially if there's a long history there. If your new friend becomes controlling or overly needy, or tries to coax you into shifty behavior that you don't feel comfortable with, it's time to take a break and reassess your friendship.

If your friends start acting like villains, call 'em out.

Actions, not words, are what matter. A friend may tell you she's always there, that she stashes your secrets in a locked vault, that she'd drive into a pit of molten lava or swallow a hundred habanero peppers for you. But if you find out the person you've confided in is sharing your secrets with everyone she meets, she's a ninja, and you might not be as close or valued as you thought.

// Stay sweet! Don't ever change!

Maybe the most important aspect of making friends is having confidence in who you are and what you believe. This comes back to identity and being confident and secure in who you are (see Chapter 15).

If you're changing yourself to fit in, stop. I mean it.

Sure, every friendship requires sacrifice, but if you find yourself behaving differently or compromising your convictions, things will get weird. Remember, you're dominating your own world here, and you have no need for vampires, ninjas, or zombies. There's nothing wrong with following when following is called for, or listening to other perspectives (aka getting advice), but if you're just blindly stumbling along in search of acceptance, others will see that, and you won't earn their respect. You'll get used.

Besides, a true friend won't end a friendship simply because you think or act differently. You might get teased or mocked on the surface, but in truth, your friends will respect you more.

// Be a friend

The easiest way to get others on your side is to treat them with kindness. This even works with people who aren't kind to you. Maybe they treat you like crap, but if you respond with kindness, eventually they'll either give up or turn around and be your friend. Even Kobe Bryant figured this out, and he won an NBA championship after realizing he needed the players around him. Contrary to what the old saying says, experience shows that nice guys don't finish last.

// Realize you don't know everything

Old people are always going on about how the more they know, the more they realize they don't know. It can get annoying, I know.

There's an important lesson there, though. When we understand our limitations and what we don't know, it frees us to seek the support of others. It makes us less arrogant and more likable. Listening is an underrated skill, and absorbing the wisdom of others protects us from making some of the same mistakes.

Making mistakes is part of any process, to be sure, but if you're familiar with the experience of others, you'll be on your toes and prepared for what's coming, and the mistakes won't morph into disasters. Learning from the experiences of others gives you a mental edge.

// Allies, honesty, and the necessity of conflict

It is not always easy to accept, but the most valuable friends we have are the ones who call us out, who are willing to stand up to us when we are wrong.

They're the heroes strong enough to face us when we're acting like a villain . . . or a fool.

In our lives, it is conflict—not success or reward—that helps us become better. When we surround ourselves with allies who understand this and have the courage to speak up when we are out of line, we are better off than if we had a hundred yes-men.

A true friend doesn't just criticize, though. A true friend helps show us the error of our ways, but also reaches down to pull us out of the holes we dig for ourselves and encourages us to overcome whatever obstacles we face.

True friends don't compete against us; they journey with us.

18.

How to Dominate
the Dating Scene

You want to find the perfect guy or the perfect girl and to be
generally well liked by the opposite sex? First, forget what you've
been told.

Dating is like Cambodia: It's littered with land mines and
there are a lot of poisonous bugs and snakes, but it's also beautiful,
and you'll have experiences you've never imagined.

Maybe that's a weird analogy.

The point is, our dating relationships are marked with tower-
ing highs and devastating lows. Falling in love can teach us in-

credible lessons in kindness, empathy, love, and putting others above ourselves. Relationships can also expose our dark sides (jealousy, anger, and envy).

I don't mean to make dating sound so severe, but it often seems so fun and frivolous that we forget the pain of heartbreak or the hard work a healthy relationship takes.

OK, not to get all "men are from Mars, women are from Venus" on you, but the way men and women approach relationships is vastly different. Because of that gap, I'm going to separate this chapter into two distinct parts. Girls, I think you'll still learn a lot from reading the guys' part, and guys, you'll definitely want to tune into what I'm gonna say to the girls, so no skipping through parts of the chapter, ya hear me?

Ordinarily I'd say "ladies first," but I think the guys really need a good talkin' to, so we'll start with the gentlemen . . .

// Dating Advice for Dudes

There's this guy who goes by the name "Mystery" (his real name is Erik von Markovik). Mystery wears feather boas and shiny clothes, and he sometimes wears a cowboy hat and, for reasons he explains, aviator goggles. Mystery has a show on VH1 called *The Pickup Artist,* where he and a greasy-looking buddy teach nerdy guys how to pick up ladies.

He's spent a significant portion of his life learning how to get women to sleep with him and he probably deserves a swift kick to the pants. He's also really, really proud of himself. (Feel free to shudder here.)

Whatever you want to say about Mystery, what he does works. He'll walk into a bar—or a grocery store or a Laundromat—and walk out with a woman.

What Mystery has learned, and what he teaches the weirdos on his reality show, is how to fake his way through the courting process.

Instead of confidence, Mystery coaches insecure guys on how to feign cockiness. Instead of a genuine sense of humor and wit, Mystery advocates a series of prerehearsed lines to alternately tear a woman down and then build her back up. Instead of advocating a powerful sense of unique self, Mystery instructs his charges to wear crazy clothes in order to help spark conversation. In essence, Mystery has become highly proficient in imitating what a man should be.

This is why it always seems . . .

// The best girls only date jerks

Jerks, for all their inherent jerkiness, also display a convincing outward show of power and confidence. Pirates are often willing to go to the most extravagant lengths to "win" the best girls . . . but they're just after her booty. Literally. They charm, they pillage, they disappear. And they leave the best girls in ruins.

Chances are, when it comes to girls, you look for certain things. Sure, you want to date someone who's funny, intelligent, and laughs at your jokes. But if you're honest, you also want to date someone who's hot.

There's nothing wrong with that. I don't know why we're wired that way, but that's how it is.

But here's the thing: Girls don't operate the same way. They care about physical appearance, sure. They want you to smell decent and have cool shoes. What they really want, though, is a guy who is confident, who knows himself. They want someone who makes them laugh. If that guy looks like Robert Pattinson or Johnny Depp, all the better. But truth be told, it's far from essential. Guys, on the other hand, are far more willing to ignore single-digit SAT scores and a bland sense of humor (at least to some extent) for a pretty face. Girls are not. If you're a boring, mopey oaf, you're dead in the water. Even if your hair looks good.

It's important to realize this for one simple, spectacular reason:

// No girl is out of your league

Allow me to repeat that. *No girl is out of your league.* Got it? You might want to read that sentence out loud to ensure that it sinks in.

Now, I'm not saying that every girl is going to like you, but you'd be surprised. Any girl worth her salt isn't going to care if you have a six-pack and are captain of the

> ### Awesomeness Tip
> Be the kind of person your ideal girlfriend (or boyfriend) would want to be with. There's no point looking for the "perfect" someone if that someone wouldn't ever be looking for someone like you.

lacrosse team. She's going to like you if you're confident, interesting, and have good character.

I have a friend in high school who never dated. He had crushes on girls, but he was deathly afraid of rejection.

It's hard to blame him. Rejection is painful. There's nothing quite so terrifying as telling someone you like her, only to get your heart stomped on by the dreaded "I just see you as a friend."

Years later, through Facebook and mutual friends, my friend found out the three girls he'd been the most interested in in high school would've dated him in a gnome's heartbeat. (That's faster than a regular heartbeat, because gnomes are small.) Because of my friend's fear of rejection, he missed three chances at getting to know those girls more.

Wearing aviator goggles will not get you a girlfriend. Wearing body sprays that reek of cedar chips and rhino musk will not get you a girlfriend. Driving a Porsche will not get you a girlfriend. Dressing in flashy shirts, spiking your hair, and tanning until you're peanut-colored will not get you a girlfriend (well, it might, but not the kind of girl you're going to like being around in another month).

Here's what *will* get you a girlfriend:

—Be confident in yourself

If you carry yourself with self-assurance, girls will look at you instantly and think, "There's something different about that guy." Self-assurance is not cockiness. It doesn't mean bragging about how awesome you are, or how many one-armed push-ups you can do with a small child balanced on your back. It means having a strong character and being certain of who you are. It comes back to your sense of identity, to being a hero that dominates his own world. We all have self-doubt at times, but true confidence overshadows that.

—Be interesting . . . and interested

Let your sense of humor show. Be quick-witted. If a girl teases you playfully, tease her playfully back (though you should never be outright mean or rude). Again, the key word here is "confidence." The more you know about a wide range of topics, the easier you can converse. Even more important, LISTEN. Ask questions and pay attention to the answers. Treat them like they're more important than you, 'cause that's what heroes do—put others before themselves.

—Be clean

You don't need to smell like cheap aftershave and wear the finest loafers made of imported rabbit skin, but you should at least be presentable. Wear clothes that fit your frame, and for Pete's sake, wear deodorant. Don't be that dude with a ten-foot radius of empty space around him at all times because he's too clueless to keep his pits odor-free. Shave. Call me superficial, but the only woman I met who was into wispy mustaches had a wispy mustache herself, and that's just plain creepy. Brush. Floss. Nothing is less attractive than a dude with horrible breath.

—Put yourself out there

If you want to make a friend (or a stranger) a girlfriend, you have to be willing to take risks. Don't give way to fear. Fear is the mind-killer.

It's up to you to analyze that risk, though. When a girl is interested, she gives off signals. When you're young, these signals are much harder to see, but they're there. My friend who had those three crushes in high school couldn't ever figure out why one of the girls always sat incredibly close to him, or put her hand on his arm when she laughed. He figured she just didn't know about personal space. The takeaway lesson: If a girl laughs at your jokes, looks at you a little too often, or finds excuses to physically touch you a lot, there is a very good chance she's into you. If she plays with her hair, same thing. If she actively tries to kiss your neck, that's probably a sign, too, though it's an oddly aggressive one.

Sometimes you gotta be the one to make the first move and, again, be confident about it. Don't just lurk around, sneak glances at her, and dance around the issue in conversation. You'll probably just creep her out. Don't be a stalker; be a man.

—Be a man of character

This one may not show instant results, but it's the most important thing you can do. If you make a promise, keep it. If you say you're going to be somewhere, be there. Be someone your girlfriend (or prospective girlfriend) can rely on. Don't be a flake. Don't let her walk all over you. Treat her with honor. When you make mistakes, own up to them. It may seem like it takes too much work, but trust me, it will work out in the long term.

// Not every girl will get it

Let's say you do all these things, and you treat a girl great, and she still just isn't into you.

Then it's time to move on. Not every girl you meet is going to be ready for a healthy relationship, no matter how hard you try. Some girls, sadly, *want* to date jerks. They've got ghosts to deal with. Let them fight those battles. Regardless of what romantic comedies say, you can't force someone into liking you. All you can do is hope she doesn't get hurt too bad, and maybe it can work out someday. Sorry, but she's a classic puppy dog . . . even the cutest, funnest girl in the world may be more trouble than she's worth, at least for now. It may be painful, and it may go against everything your hormones are screaming at you, but it's time to move on. You've got better things to do. Sayonara, puppy.

// Dating Advice for the Ladies

The best advice on dating I ever heard for women was from a college professor named Randy Pausch. Randy was dying from cancer when he gave his "Last Lecture," one of the most inspirational speeches I've ever heard. You should check it out online or buy the book. Seriously. You'll be blown away.

Randy's advice to his daughter, who was two years old at the time, boiled everything down into one sentence:

"When men are romantically interested in you, it's really simple. Just ignore everything they say and only pay attention to what they do."

That's it. That's all.

If you follow that advice, you'll literally never be fooled.

// Actions define a person, not words

Think about it: If a guy tells you he's funny, but never makes you laugh, is he actually funny?

Right. So why would it be any different when it comes to love? It doesn't matter if a guy *says* he loves you. If he's catching make-out sessions with fifteen other girls, it's not true. If he's treating you like crap, it's not true. If he's rude and never calls, it's not true. If he's mentally or physically abusing you—HE. DOES. NOT. LOVE. YOU.

Sorry. The truth hurts sometimes.

That's not to say guys don't make mistakes and don't deserve forgiveness. Guys actually tend to make a LOT of mistakes. We're clumsy, clueless creatures half the time. And to make things worse, we can't read your minds. But when the mistakes keep happening, it's time to get out. It doesn't matter what you think about yourself: No one deserves to be treated poorly. If you think you somehow deserve to be treated badly, you are wrong. The ghosts are lying to you, and the pirates in your life need to walk the plank.

It's not always easy to tell if you're dating a vampire or a puppy or a ninja, so you might need a clearer perspective. Find someone you trust and look up to, preferably someone who doesn't know your significant other that well, and talk to them about what's going on. If that person hears all the pluses and minuses about your boyfriend and tells you to run, do yourself a favor: Run.

By the way,

// Cheaters never prosper

And by that I mean, if a guy is cheating on his girlfriend with you, (a) it is very likely he will cheat on you. He may treat you all nice now, but he's a scumbag. He doesn't have a moral backbone. He doesn't know how to commit or be faithful. He's a villain. And, (b) WHAT THE HECK ARE YOU DOING MAKING OUT WITH SOME OTHER GIRL'S BOYFRIEND, YOU BACKSTABBING NINJA!

> *Awesomeness Tip*
> Contrary to popular belief, people—even if they're very much in love—cannot read one another's minds. Open communication of thoughts, feelings, and expectations is absolutely critical.

Sorry, that was louder than I intended. But seriously, stop it. You're embarrassing yourself and hurting other people and definitely breaking Rule Number 2.

Back to cheaters. If a guy has cheated on you once, it is very likely he will do it again. Think of it as the opposite of our legal system: A cheater is guilty until proven innocent. That doesn't mean a cheater can't change, but be very, very wary. Remember, actions speak louder than words here. Don't defend him as "a really great guy" until he's proved he actually is a really great guy.

// Hold out for a hero

Don't just settle for the first guy to take interest in you. I know sometimes good girls like you worry that you'll get overlooked somehow. That the prettier, easier vampire girls will seduce all the good guys and ruin them forever. That if you don't hurry up and date somebody—anybody—you'll end up alone. Like, forever.

Don't worry. It's like I told the guys: In the end, it's character that counts. Scoring dates and developing the character required for a long-term, committed relationship are completely different skill sets.

That said, let's say you're interested in a guy, but you don't know if he's interested in you. For thirty days, put yourself on his radar. Talk to him at school. Chat with him online. Drop him a super-casual message on Facebook or MySpace. If you have mutual friends, try and find situations where you can hang out in groups. If he doesn't ask you out or state his interest in those thirty days, move on. It's possible he's not interested, but it's also possible he doesn't have the courage. If it's the former, you won't have to suffer the embarrassment of being turned down (call me old-fashioned, but I think guys should take the majority of the risks in these situations). If he doesn't have the guts to ask you out, then maybe it'll happen later. Either way, you've done your part.

No matter what, do not change yourself to get a guy to like you. That's a ninja/vampire thing to do, and often, you'll just end up playing into the hands of a pirate. It's OK to take interest in his interests, but any man who doesn't like you for who you are doesn't deserve your time. You should always expect to be treated well, but the best way to assure that is to be yourself. If a guy can't handle that, move on.

Alright, now let's bring everyone back together for a few coed thoughts. NO CANOODLING!!! You there, in the back, stop whispering! I'm about to drop some knowledge bombs.

// On sex

As a married man with a beautiful wife, let me tell you: There are few things in life better than sex. Anyone who tells you otherwise is a lunatic, or at least has some very serious issues (in which case, you should not call them a lunatic—that's insensitive . . . and potentially dangerous to your health).

(NOTE: If you're reading this and you're like, "Sex? Ha-ha! Josh uses such silly words! I wonder what it means . . . ?" this is one of those times when it's probably best not to go ask Google. Put this book down, go find your parents, and ask them to explain it. That'll probably make them really uncomfortable, but too bad; it's about time you heard it from them. It beats me why people try to keep sex such a secret.)

OK, back to our regularly scheduled programming. I say sex is great, and it is. But here's the thing: Sex is just one part of life; it isn't life itself. A lot of the vampires out there today would have you believe that sex is the whole point of life, that life revolves around when you have sex and how often and with whom. That's crazy.

Let me put it this way: If you're having a crappy week and everything in your life feels like it's falling apart, and you have amazing sex . . . that doesn't change the fact that you've had a crappy week. All your other problems don't just go away. And if you're having a great week and everything's going just perfect, and you have lame sex (sorry to break your heart, kids; it happens), that's NOT going to ruin your week.

What I'm saying is this: In the grand scheme of things, sex is probably overrated. Having sex won't "make you a man" or turn you into an Angelina Jolie–grade seductress, or make you more mature or magically fix your self-esteem issues. It just won't.

This probably sounds crazy to you, and I don't blame you. If I tried telling that to seventh-grade me I would've laughed in my own face.

Sex was pretty much one of the only things the boys I knew talked about in seventh grade. And you better believe I was interested. You see, in seventh grade, I joined band. I played the trombone, mostly because I liked the idea of being able to spit on the floor and have that be okay. I got pretty good and became first chair. And from my seat in that first chair, I was in an absolute prime position for staring at Christina. If I squinted my eyes just right in feigned concentration, I could stare at Christina where she sat, playing the clarinet, for what seemed like eternities at a time, and no one could tell.

She was a year older than me, and she was *hot*. Something welled up in me, something I hadn't felt before. I longed to tell her everything about me, all about who I was and wanted to be. I wanted to tell her the mystery of my mother, the tragedy of my grandfather's death, the aroma of sweet barbecue mingling with dust during an evening watermelon festival—maybe even the emptiness of a foster home where your chief value is the monthly check your presence brings. I wanted to tell her all of it because I knew, somehow, that if I could bring myself to do it—and if she'd let me—she would know from the witness of my eyes that it was true and that we were meant to be together forever.

I knew I couldn't say all that. I had never even spoken to Christina aside from the customary "Hi" when we'd awkwardly approach the band-room door at the same time, and one of us had to go in first (of course I'd let her go first). But I daydreamed a lot.

When I wasn't in class, I sometimes gathered in the halls with other seventh-grade boys, who always talked about their sexual exploits. Never mind that the seventh graders at my school didn't have "exploits"; only a couple of them had kissed a girl for real I bet, outside of a game of spin the bottle. That didn't stop them from talking, though.

"Sure, I've had sex," one would say. "I've gotten some, like, a dozen times."

"No you haven't."

"Yeah I did."

"With who?"

"You don't know her. She's really hot, though. I went to camp with her this summer."

The others were skeptical. "What's her name?"

He would give a name. "She's a year older than us." The year-older detail was important. Saying you'd hooked up with a sixth-grader? One point. A seventh-grader? Two points. An eighth-grader? That was like, 100 points.

"I think I might know who you're talking about."

"No, no, not her. Another girl. Another one. From camp."

"Who then?"

"Oh . . . I don't know her last name."

"You had sex with a girl and you don't know her last name? Yeah right, you're full of it."

The boy would insist he was telling the truth and the rest of us would call him a liar. The more details a boy could provide for his story, the more credible it was, and if no one could catch him in a lie, he gained the ultimate badge of authority: The right to give everyone else advice on how to get girls.

Finally one day it became my turn, and I was completely unprepared.

"What about you, Josh?" one of the boys said. "You're not a virgin, are you?"

I had never even kissed a girl—couldn't remember if I'd even held hands, tell the truth—but I couldn't tell these guys; all the social capital I had earned through a whole semester of cracking jokes and playing pranks would be lost forever. "Of course I'm not," I snorted. "I just don't have to brag about it like you guys."

My hope was that my confidence would convince them to change the subject or at least turn their attention to someone else, but no luck. They did seem willing to believe me, but that just made them hungrier for details. The boys instinctively huddled in closer. "Who was it?" one asked.

"This girl," I said, my mind racing, "in my band class. She's an eighth grader. Pretty hot. Nice bod."

All the boys froze, as if reviewing my band roster in their heads. Uh-oh. How could they know who was in band? I suddenly remembered one of them had an older brother who played oboe. And there were few enough girls in my middle school with developed bodies that they actually had a shot at picking her out from my description. I started to regret my lie.

"Blonde or brunette?"

"Brunette."

"What's her name?"

I decided to give up. "Look, I'm not going to tell you her name. She came over my house, we hooked up, we did it. That's all I'm going to say."

The boys started to call me out for lying, when one of them looked across at me with a grin. "I know who it is," he said.

"No, you don't."

"Yeah, I do." The others hushed. "There's only three hot eighth-grade girls in band, and only one of them's a brunette, dude."

He was right. Of course he was right. That's part of the reason I stared at her all the time, and none of the other girls in the room.

"You got some from Christina? Aw, man. How did you do that?"

I was caught in the lie, completely busted, so . . . I kept digging. I made up a story about how I invited Christina back to my place, nobody was home, she let me take her shirt off, I felt her up, and we had sex. I filled in details where I could, which wasn't often because I had no idea what I was talking about. Mostly I regurgitated little bits of stories I'd heard from other boys. I made them promise not to tell anyone, and they gave a solemn oath.

Obviously I didn't understand how a rumor mill works. Within two days, I was in trouble.

"Are you Josh Shipp?"

Four large eighth-graders waited for me as I came in from lunch. They looked unhappy and, naive as I was, I couldn't imagine why. I didn't know these guys at all, and had no idea why they were invading my personal space like this.

"Yeah?" I said.

"Did you tell people you had sex with Christina?"

I panicked when the ringleader said her name.

". . . No?" I offered, but I might as well have said yes. Terror painted the guilt on my face.

"Dude, you're dead," he hissed, poking a finger into my chest. "Christina's a good friend of mine; she's a cool girl. After band class, dude. After band class. As soon as we see you, you are so dead. Don't even try to run."

He shoved me and they stalked away, glaring at me over their shoulders. I felt sick. He was right—there was no point in running. Those guys were big, looked like they were into lifting weights already, and could certainly catch me even faster than they could beat the snot out of me.

I thought about letting them beat me up, but couldn't stand the thought of the four of them working me over and humiliating me in front of the whole school (again), and telling everyone why they did it. I'd go home like that, and I'd have to tell Grandma that I lied. Lied about somebody else, and gotten beaten up for it. She'd be so disappointed. Maybe she'd think I finally got what I deserved for telling lies about people. No, I couldn't let them beat me up.

Could I talk my way out of it? Only by going to Christina, in hopes she would call them off. Fat chance. Heck, maybe she would jump in and help them! I told people I had sex with her! She must have known by then if those guys knew, and she must have hated me. How could I ever look her in the face again, much less ask her for protection?! What kind of a sissy would do that anyway?

That left just one option. They said as soon as they see me, I'm so dead. I had to make sure they'd never see me. So I never went to sixth-period band class again.

Instead, each day, I waited until the moment before the sixth-period bell rang and ducked into the boys' bathroom near the back of the school and hid in a stall. I waited for about ten minutes; then, after checking that the coast was clear, I ran for the outside door. There were fifty yards of open playground field where someone might see me, so I had to run hard and make for a concrete drainage ditch that provided cover while I stole toward home.

Those vengeful eighth graders never beat me up. But the regret did. That stupid lie ruined seventh grade. And I told that lie to try to fit in with the vampires and their empty promises.

Let me be straight with you: If you spend your life trying to get girls (or lie about getting girls, like me) to make yourself feel better, or you dress sexy and flirt with guys to fit in or be popular, you're going to end up disappointed. You're chasing a lie.

You're also playing with a puppy I'm willing to bet you're no-where near ready to purchase.

Whether you want to admit it or not, sex comes with a serious emotional impact. There is no such thing as no-strings-attached sexual contact, no matter what anyone says. Sometimes you might think you've gotten away with something, 'cause it's possible you won't feel the impact or notice any consequences right away, but trust me, you will. And, even worse, the other person is often hurt, too. So don't be a pirate, OK?

I still remember getting the "sex talk." Gary had come over to take me grocery shopping, and then we'd cook at his place. Gary wasn't related to me or anything, but he was basically like my grown-up older brother. Good guy. One of the first guys in my life who made me feel like I mattered, you know? As I ran to my room to get ready, he and Grandma spoke in hushed tones in the kitchen. I suspected nothing.

At the grocery store we walked the aisles as we had several times before, and I cracked jokes about strange foods and brand names, expecting him to join in. Gary was oddly silent, though. It was as if he were sure he had forgotten something and was trying to recall what it was; or perhaps he had a bad day at work. We hauled the bags out to his car, which we called the "green tank," and put them in the trunk. When we climbed into the front seats, he didn't start the car.

I could hear Gary's breathing before he turned to me. It paused, then started again.

"Now, Jamie, your grandma wanted us to have kind of a conversation about something I may need to kind of inform you of. . . . Now, do you know . . . I mean . . . um . . . well . . . ?"

As Gary fumbled for words, I realized what was happening. Oh, for Pete's sake, he's going to have the sex talk with me!

I stiffened, hoping it could somehow just be over. I had figured I would escape the sex talks other kids endured, because I couldn't imagine my grandma could get through it without fainting. I knew the basics about sex—a man and a woman, and all the anatomy involved. Of course there was more I wanted to know, but I couldn't imagine asking, partly because the mere mention of sex made adults stutter and turn ghostly white.

"Now, when a man and a woman love each other . . . are you familiar with the term 'making love'?"

I nodded my head in no particular direction, crosswise maybe, as if to say, "I acknowledge what you say, but I'm not going to answer."

"It's a good idea to wait. You want to make sure it's serious—the relationship; that you're ready," he said. "I waited for a long time, and there's nothing wrong with that."

This I hadn't heard before; and if I got one valuable thing from the talk, this was it. In my conversations with the boys at school, sex was always rite of passage, a badge of honor, a milestone to be achieved as soon as possible, like R-rated movies and driving. If Gary waited, I could wait and feel okay about it. I would still have to lie to the guys, of course, but I could feel secure within myself.

And that, my friends, is the key. A lot of people have sex because they're insecure. WORST. REASON. EVER.

Sex is the cutest puppy at the pound. But do not—let me repeat and emphasize that—*do not* enter a sexual relationship lightly.
I'm not going to go on and on about your sexuality being a precious
lily-white flower, but I can assure you most of us enter into our
sexual lives without fully understanding the ramifications. Speaking of ramifications, did you know sex can lead to pregnancy, and
that pregnancy leads to babies? (Coincidence?) And even if you
don't end up birthing a baby from fooling around, you'll likely
birth a billion ghosts.

General rule: Do not compromise your beliefs on sex to make
someone else happy. If a guy or girl is going to break up with you
because you won't go as far as they like, beat them to the punch and
break up with them. They're acting like a bounty-hungry pirate
and manipulating you like a ninja. Ditch the relationship; that ship
is going down anyway. Compromising your beliefs will only lead
to pain.

I'm sure you know this, but if you do choose to enter into a
sexual relationship, use protection. Pregnancies happen. Disease is
more common than you think. Some studies claim teenagers (15–
19 years old) account for 41 percent of the 18.9 million cases of the
sexually transmitted infections diagnosed every year. If that doesn't
give you the willies, nothing will.

Your sex-ed teacher or a doctor can detail the best methods for
avoiding pregnancy and STDs, but not having sex (what fans of
big words call abstinence) is the only 100 percent guaranteed way
to stay healthy and un-knocked-up. Just sayin'.

// On pornography

I can't imagine being a teenage boy these days. Every teenage boy throughout the history of time has dealt with rampaging hormones and moments of unrestrained lust. It's a fact of adolescence—just be thankful that you didn't grow up in some tribal village with only a loincloth to cover your sensitive regions.

These days there's a lot more than seminude cave babes messing with your mind. Sexual imagery has never been more prevalent in advertising and entertainment than it is today. For proof of this, just try and go a single day without being confronted by ten examples of sex being used to sell products. I'd be surprised if you made it to 3 P.M. without going over the limit.

Now, pornography is a different matter. (Side note: Why does "pornography" sound like a science? Hmm.) No one in history has had nearly the level of access to sexual pictures and video that you do. And, contrary to what you might believe, that's nothing to celebrate.

Whatever you think about pornography, here's one thing I know from my experience: It does not help when it comes to real relationships. In fact, it hurts. A lot. Pornography creates totally false expectations about what sex is. You know the saying about comparing apples and oranges? That applies to pornography and actual sex, too. There's just no comparing the two. Pornography objectifies and cheapens an act that is important and private, and it objectifies men and women. Plus, it creates a ridiculously erroneous impression of what the human body should be. News flash: Not every woman has breasts the size of regulation basketballs; not every man has a penis the length of a baseball bat; and, if I can be frank for a moment, that's a good thing.

Here's a warning, though. Porn can be addictive. Like anything that provides a cheap thrill—Doritos, multiple shots of espresso within a short span of time—it wears off quickly and leaves you with a mental and physical hangover.

I know the temptations, but if you ask me, you're best off keeping as far away from pornography as you can. Porn is for pirates. And sad, lonely people without any self-control or dignity.

// On breaking up

It's a fact of life: Some relationships don't work. All relationships take effort and change, and they all demand that you become a better person. You can't give up every time you hit a minor road bump or get sad, but there are also times when it's clear a relationship isn't going to work. If this is the case, it's time to cut your losses and step away. No one ever said it was easy, but you'll be glad when you look back and see how a small, honest expenditure of pain prevented a much larger (and longer) one.

The best way to end a relationship is cleanly. Don't drag a breakup out over weeks and months. Explain your reasons clearly. It's very likely the other person will be hurt, so minimize the damage, and if there's no hope of getting back together, say so. Don't jerk your ex around like a five-year-old with a yo-yo.

And please, for the love of all things holy, break up in person. If that's not possible, do it over the phone. Never, ever, ever break up via e-mail or text (though you can use e-mail to articulate your thoughts later). It's thoughtless, rude, and hurtful. Not to mention cowardly as heck.

// On other fish in the sea

If you've ever been on the other end of that breakup, you know how painful it can be. It's like someone ripped off your face and smacked you in the head with it. Like being nibbled to death in slow increments by starving piranhas. Like having your intestines savaged by a grizzly. Basically, it's the feeling of your world falling apart. You might feel unloved and worthless. You'll probably feel like you should never date anyone ever again. You might even look into the possibility of becoming a nun. Breakups are some of the most painful experiences we'll ever have.

The last thing we want to hear after suffering a bad breakup—when we can hardly eat and we've been holding back tears for a week straight—is the phrase *There are other fish in the sea*. Oh, man, that's so obnoxious.

So hopefully you're not actively dealing with heartbreak when I tell you this. If you are, feel free to skip ahead and come back to it later. It'll still be here.

There are other fish in the sea.

There are other frogs in the pond.

There are other jackrabbits in the desert.

There are other hipsters in Brooklyn.

People use this annoying cliche because it's true. When you're going through a breakup, it's hard to imagine going through the process all over again: Meeting someone, getting to know them, sharing your life, falling in love. But it *does* happen, and it will be just as magical, if not more so, and maybe this time it won't end with a broken heart. The younger you are, the more likely it is you'll find someone new. When I remember my first girlfriend in high school, and recall the pain our breakup caused, it's almost funny now. It never would've worked out, but that relationship helped teach me what would work, and the relationships after that worked out better and better until I finally found my wife.

// On marriage

I know a couple who have been married for over thirty years. They met in high school and lived across the street from each other. They had three children and live near where they grew up. They have a great story.

But their story wasn't all rainbows and unicorns. Every relationship that has ever existed has been hard, and no couple stays together for ten or twenty or thirty years without conflict. The secret of a good relationship is being prepared for this, and accepting the truth that a minor conflict is just going to bring you and your partner closer in the end, provided you can deal with it adequately and play fair.

In fact, that's one of the things that makes relationships so great. My friend gave me this advice on my wedding day, right as I was donning my tuxedo jacket: "It will be the hardest thing you ever do, but as it goes on, you will look back and find you are a better person."

The married couple I mentioned were high school sweethearts who stuck together no matter what, but they are a rare exception. There's no perfect age for getting married, but you will save yourself a lot of hard work if you know yourself by the time you say "I do." If I'd married the puppy I dated in high school, my life would look awfully different now, and probably rather awful. I wouldn't have been able to follow my dreams. I wouldn't have found a woman who is an infinitely better partner and has brought me so much happiness. It would have been very, very hard.

And marriage is hard enough as is. But don't worry. It's worth it. (I love you, Sarah!)

19.

How to Dominate Your School

Dominating your school is not about being the most popular or about being the best. It's about working your tail off.

Surely I'm joking.

I swear, I'm not.

Basic formula: You have to do what you have to do in order to do what you want to do. In order to succeed with school/life/girls/boys, you have to put in the work. It's like how your parents make you get into the Brussels sprouts before you can cuddle up to some dessert. If that sounds grim, take a breath. It's not. Working for what you want always feels good. It's like phys ed for the soul.

> ## MOST COMMON FORMS OF VILLAINY IN SCHOOL
> ### VAMPIRES; ROBOTS; ZOMBIES

Memorize this:

// You don't have to live life the way other people expect you to

I'm going to lay it out as plain as can be: high school → college → marriage → 2.5 kids + a dog in the suburbs + a job you don't like = NOT necessarily the path you have to follow. "Everyone else is doing it" is generally not a great reason to hop in line. Remember, most people don't dominate their worlds. Most people aren't heroes. Ergo, most people aren't great examples to follow.

You can be whatever you want to be, do whatever you want to do.

But your options are going to be really limited if you don't start making smart decisions now.

// You've gotta think ahead

Sorry to break it to you, but your future isn't some nebulous spectacle looming in the distance. It starts today. Scratch that: It starts *now*. After all, if you don't know where you're going, how will you know when you get there? In this respect, school is more than just a minimum-security prison that serves chocolate-chip cookies on the good days. Nope, there's a lot more to it than that (even if it's hard to tell sometimes). Basically, education is about preparation for SOMETHING. Think about what you want to do. Anything: Iguana farmer, hot-air-balloon pilot, submarine captain, brain surgeon, lion tamer, cultural anthropologist, international diplomat, software developer. OK, cool. Now, ask yourself how you get there. It's like Harry Potter wanting to be an Auror, right? He had to score at a certain level on certain tests or he would be forever disqualified (or at least seriously disadvantaged). Approach your dream job with that mind-set.

And in the meantime,

// Watch out for robots

Here's the thing: School can seem like a robot factory.

From early on, you take standardized tests, filling in little bubbles, on the paper which are fed into a machine that scores the test and tells you how you rank compared to the other robots. In every class, you are assigned a letter grade, proving your proficiency (or lack of proficiency) in each subject, and this letter grade is the magical token that allows you to move up to the next level.

The best robots go to college, which are more specialized factories. Here your database is uploaded with all manners of information so you, too, can calculate how to become a productive member of robot society. If you go to the finest robot colleges, you get extra robot points, so other robots will know immediately how well programmed you are. When you graduate, you march into lines and roll over another conveyor belt, where you are given another piece of paper saying you are a successful robot. There really is no way around this, because other robots are constantly reminding you there is no other choice if you want to succeed.

After that, you receive your third robot uniform: A shirt and a tie (or a skirt if you are a girl). You bring in your pieces of paper to a job interview, where a boss robot scans them and judges you based on what the papers say. Then he asks you robotic questions, like, "Where do you see yourself in five years?" "Are you a team player?" "Do you take criticism well?" Those last two are code for "Are you a robot like us?" and "Will you do whatever we tell you?"

If you answer these questions in a way that computes positively to the boss robot, you will receive your job. You will be told when to arrive and what you will be doing. You will power on every morning and make your way diligently to giant holding bays, sometimes with tiny, sectioned-off robot rooms without ceilings or doors, so other robots can make sure you are operating properly. You will set about producing, staying consistent. Here you'll be programmed to utter robot sayings. When other robots ask you how you are on a Monday, you absolutely must say, "What can I say? It's a Monday." If it's a Thursday, you must say, "What can

I say? Thursday is almost Friday." Don't even get me started on the phrase "hump-day." It's not as fun as it sounds.

But at any point, you can just turn your life around, right? You could quit and go do whatever you like! Sort of . . . but eventually, it'll be too late to do anything else, and the programming will take over. You might even make excuses for yourself, saying it wasn't your fault that you ended up where you did. After all, you just followed the program given to you. Oh, sure, you might experience some tiny glitches in the program here and there. They're usually called midlife crises. A midlife crisis is a feeling that you have to get out, start living for your passions, make something of yourself, leave a legacy with your life. Most robots don't follow this instinct. They just buy a fast car to feel young again. But soon enough, you'll be back on the productive track, numbly plugging your way through another robot day.

Truth be told, the world needs robots. It needs people to do mindless, excruciatingly dull work. How else will all that data be inputted? How else will those reports be generated and filed correctly? How else will the phones get answered in the correct order they were received? How else will the time clocks be stamped and the correct monetary credits distributed to the correct robots efficiently? If you're lucky, maybe you'll get a few extra credits, so you can buy bright, shiny robot accessories!

There's always the chance you might short-circuit and break down one day. More likely, though, you'll be replaced by the cheaper, faster, updated model. You'll eventually be removed from service, sent to the trash heap with, hopefully, enough credits to last a few more years. It won't matter, though, because you'll have spent so much time being a robot, you won't be programmed to do anything else.

Not to worry, though. There's still work to be done. The robot holding bay will keep going as if you were never there.

Depressing, huh?

That's not to say school or college is bad, or that you're doomed to end up a robot. Most of the time, some form of education is critical for successful world domination.

Here's my point: In your education—whether in high school, trade school, college, or grad school—you've gotta . . .

// Keep your eye on the goal

A lot of times you've gotta do what you have to do in order to do what you want. If you want to be a pilot, you've gotta learn to fly a plane. You want to run a company, you're probably going to want to acquire a few business or management skills.

Never jump through hoops just because someone tells you to. But if the quickest, most logical way to get to your goal is to jump through hoops . . . well, so be it. Sometimes hoops need jumping through.

One of those hoops is school.

Education can make you feel like one of those yippy dogs in agility competitions. You yearn to run free through the woods, chasing squirrels and bounding through an open meadow after butterflies. Instead, you're stuck in some bizarro dog-show competition, with a demanding owner who dresses you in human clothes and forces you to run up and down ramps and through canvas tunnels for a treat.

The fact is,

// Education is necessary

I'm not just saying that because I have to say it or schools will stop inviting me to speak. I'm saying that because it's true. I'll give you three reasons:

—Reason #1: Paper

My friend Mindy spent four years earning her bachelor's degree, three years working for a doctorate in physical therapy, and four years in medical school. In exchange, she has three pieces of paper.

Don't get me wrong, they're fancy pieces of paper, with gold stamps and signatures. They are also pieces of paper the same way keys are pieces of metal—they unlock doors.

Those pieces of paper do not prove you are smart. They don't prove moral strength or physical prowess or a brilliant sense of humor.

What a diploma proves is that you are willing to work hard.

That's why so many jobs require college degrees, and why most every other job out there requires at least a high school diploma. A degree shows that a person is willing to bear down and get the work done, to spend hours studying a subject they're not interested in. It proves they are prepared to do what it takes to follow their dream.

—Reason #2: You might actually learn something

Like the dog in an agility competition, we can view our education in two ways. We can view it as a prison, a seemingly endless series of rituals and hoops intended to mold us into what society deems appropriate.

Or we can view it as training to make us better, and when we do finally hit that open meadow, we'll be able to make the most of our experience. Now you can spend all of your time sprinting and frolicking through the wildflowers.

—Reason #3: It's good for your brain

Education—the whole process of packing your head with various quantities of useful and sometimes not-so-useful information—generally makes you smarter. Not necessarily because of all the stuff you know, but because you've actually had to THINK to get the work done.

So even if you don't give a squirrel's fluffy tail about geometric proofs or neoclassical art, at the end of the day, if you've done your homework, your brain probably works a little better.

WORLD DOMINATION CHALLENGE

Are you willing to live the next two to three years of your life like most people won't so you can live the next twenty to thirty years like many people never will? In other words . . . are you willing to do what you HAVE to do in order to do exactly what you WANT? If you can answer "yes" to that question, what types of things can you do in the next two to three years to make progress?

// Well-rounded is overrated, but it still helps

Along the way, even when it comes to subjects we don't care about, we learn perspective. We can do this by looking for connections to subjects we are interested in. Maybe you couldn't give a rip about how early twentieth-century diplomacy and ethnic tensions in the Balkan states ignited World War I, but there are lessons in history that could lead you to fresh angles in programming or medicine or any other career field.

At the very least, a wide range of knowledge enables you to communicate better.

I've never been a fan of math. Outside of tip calculations and tax filings, I don't use it much.

Years ago, I read a book called *Zero: The Biography of a Dangerous Idea,* by Charles Seife. The book talked about the history of the number zero. Long ago, humans didn't see things in terms of zero. In fact, zero was considered evil. There was no reason for zero. Either you had something or you didn't. If someone asked you how much land you owned, you wouldn't say, "I have zero land." They'd probably drown you for being a witch if you said it like that.

Fortunately, the book didn't have much math, but it was still about numbers.

Since then, I've met a number of people who relished math in school the way I relished making smart aleck comments to the teacher. On the surface, we haven't had much in common, so I'll bring up that book, and it usually sparks a fascinating conversation. The book connected my interests (history) to subjects in my blind spot (math), and now links me to great friends I never would've known otherwise. Everybody wins.

// Hey! Teachers! Leave those kids alone!

Of course, education isn't always fun. We've all had teachers who drone on and on with the enthusiasm of a stoned tree sloth, or courses that threaten to drown us in assigned writing and homework.

Bad teachers are the most difficult pitfall, so I suggest avoiding them altogether if it's within your power (and hey, sometimes it's not). Ask around for suggestions on professors and teachers who are particularly skilled, and get a jump on scheduling them, since they'll likely be popular.

When it comes to difficult classes, though, don't dismiss them. Sometimes the hardest classes are the best. My friend Sean was not particularly good at school. He graduated from high school with a 2.6 GPA, even though he had higher SAT scores than anyone I knew.

His senior year, he took an honors English class that was widely considered the hardest course in the school. During summer break, the teacher required the students read four books from a list, including *The Fountainhead* by Ayn Rand. *The Fountainhead,* in case you haven't read it, is 311,596 pages long (approximately ten times longer than this book). It's about an architect, and most of it focuses on a philosophical concept known as Objectivism. There are no gunfights, only one explosion, and a very weird sex scene. Tough read.

During the year, the class read through twelve Shakespeare plays, and had three essays due weekly, along with a series of other books. It was the hardest class Sean had ever taken, and far harder than anything I've ever studied.

At the end of the semester, in a class of thirty honors students, only three people earned an A. Sean, who had averaged a C over the span of his high school career, was one of them.

It wasn't until years later that Sean decided he wanted to be a writer, but that grueling class was one of his biggest inspirations. For a guy who was awful at busywork, the kick to the head his honors English class provided was just what he needed.

// If you can't be just another brick in the wall

Some people are suited to study, to plow through a mountain of homework without a moment of procrastination. They churn out straight A's like a conveyor belt. They aren't necessarily robots, they're just extremely good at directing their brain functions toward one particular goal.

To others, the school system just doesn't seem to work. (My hand is up right now, FYI. ADD, class clown, a little chubby, bullied a lot—school was a treat for me, but I survived.) We're all different, and big public and private schools can seem suited only for the select few who would love nothing more than to read textbooks on a Saturday night. Guys like my friend Sean, who is one of the smartest people I know, can slip through the cracks.

If you're worried you're one of those people, you should remember there are other options. You should speak to your academic counselors first, but if your public or private school just doesn't seem to be working, there are all sorts of alternative learning programs or schools that focus on more individual learning habits. If you're not sure what approach to take, talk to your parents openly about your fears about your education.

Not every school is a robot factory, especially when you stand out as an individual.

20.

How to Dominate
Your Career

Raise your hand if you really want to work in a factory. (Pauses to count.) OK, you guys, go pursue that. The rest of you, figure out what you want . . . and start planning for that future now.

The average adult person is awake for fourteen to sixteen hours per day. For half that time, the average person is working at a job. There are obvious exceptions. Some people have to work two jobs just to get by. Some people live off trust funds, and do nothing but swim through gold-plated vaults of personal wealth all day, Scrooge-style. Some people live in their parents' basement until their mom kicks them out.

Doing the math from above, we see the average person sleeps about 33 percent of their life. If you factor in weekends, this means the average American spends 34 percent of his or her waking life at work.

That's a huge chunk of your life, 34 percent. If we are going to seriously discuss dominating your world, you better believe that you are going to have to dominate your career. If you don't, that 34 percent will be painful and boring. And more specifically, it will be 34 percent of your life that you spend doing the tasks of your robot bosses.

> *MOST COMMON FORMS OF VILLAINY AT WORK*
> ROBOTS; NINJAS; ZOMBIES

This chapter will explain how to dominate your career. Pay attention, 'cause this is a big one—34 percent big.

// When I grow up, I DON'T want to be a . . .

When you're young, it's easy to say you want to be a fireman or a princess, because those seem to be the only options. But the older you get, the more things open up, and the more confusing choosing a path becomes. Think of all the thousands of jobs out there. Then think about all the variations on each of those jobs. You can't just be a teacher or a doctor. You have to know which subject you'll teach and what grade. Or you'll have to know which minute segment of the body you're going to practice medicine on, like the brain or the toenails. And those are just two possible careers. It's enough to make you curl up in a corner and weep for the end.

What's worse, there's so much pressure to decide RIGHT NOW.

Not later. Now! The way your teach-bots and counsel-bots talk, what you eat for lunch any given day could permanently banish you from a decent college, which will keep you out of your perfect job, which means that no one will ever love you because you are miserable and you'll end up sitting on a sidewalk, completely homeless, remembering that fateful day you chose the sloppy joe over the chicken sandwich.

Easy, tiger. Here's the truth. They're a little bit right. The decisions you make now, from the grades you get to how you treat others, affect your options down the road. It's definitely not the end of the line if you turn off course, but knowing where you're going gives you an huge advantage, because you're thinking about steps others aren't. Or as the Cheshire Cat in *Alice in Wonderland* says, if you don't know where you are going, then "it doesn't matter which way you go."

Here's how to get out of that fetal position, brush yourself off, and start moving:

// Think backward

I know, it's weird. But think about it.

Say there are four jobs in the world. You can be a princess, a fireman, or a badger wrangler, or you can clean out toilets for a living.

If you're a dude, you can't be a princess. It just won't happen, no matter how many times you kiss a toad. See how easy that was to cross off the list? That leaves fireman, badger wrangler, and toilet cleaner. Do you like toilets? Do you like dealing with human excrement? I didn't think so.

Voilà. Your choices have been cut in half. Now, what do you like better: Running into burning buildings or training badgers to become actors on the big and small screen? It's that simple.

OK, it's not that simple, but it's a start. It's not as if you can list every job in the world and scratch them out one by one. Think of it more broadly than that. Can you see yourself working in an office, or would you rather be outside? Are you comfortable working for a boss, or do you want to run your own business? Hey, if you can't see yourself working for someone else, you've crossed off a lot of potential careers, my friend.

WORLD DOMINATION CHALLENGE

To find out what you DO want to do with your life, you have to find out what you don't want to do with your life. Take a minute, and list five (or more) things you know you never, ever, want to do with your life. Be specific! If you can do five, list five more! Keep going as long as you can!

// Pay to play?

Now that we've eliminated jobs like pizza delivery boy and garbageman (though garbagemen tend to make a great living, and pizza delivery isn't a bad gig when you're young), it's time to explore what careers are left.

To do that, you'll have to consider what you're good at. You also need to consider what you enjoy doing. This isn't quite as easy as it sounds, because you might really enjoy eating junk food all night and playing Call of Duty 4. Think more about what you feel fulfilled by. Maybe it's drawing, music, math, or speaking in front of others. It's when something is so fun, you don't consider it work, even if others do.

That's how you break free of the robot mentality. The robot mentality tells you your career should be "work." Robots tell you to work your fingers to the bone for eight hours a day in return for a tiny paycheck. Robots tell you to have fun when you're clocked out, never on company time.

What they won't tell you (because they don't want to admit it to themselves) is that there are people out there making money doing exactly what they love. There are people out there using their drawing skills to chart out buildings or to sketch comic books. There are rock stars and country musicians and teen pop sensations. There are mathematicians doing . . . whatever it is awesome mathematicians do. There are people like me who used to be class clowns, now getting paid money to speak at schools, the same places I used to get kicked out of! There are even people getting paid to chug Mountain Dew and play Call of Duty 4. They may die young, but they will die happy.

This is the Ultimate Goal.

If you want to be a guitar player, you need to play your guitar. A lot. More than anyone else. It doesn't matter if you don't know two chords when you start, because you will if you work at it. Eventually, you're going to get so good, people will have to pay you. Honestly, they'll look at you and they'll be jealous and they'll say, "Well, I suppose I have to give you this sack of cash. You're just too good." And remember, playing guitar doesn't mean you have to be packing out full stadiums on an international tour. It could mean that you get to be a studio musician, a songwriter who writes for other musicians, a guitar teacher, an artist who helps write songs for sound tracks of movies . . . the options are endless.

Sometimes this means you won't be well rounded. I mean, no one expects LeBron James to be an expert at algebra or seventeenth-century Middle Eastern politics. People expect LeBron James to ball. Does that mean he can be a jerk and blow off everything but basketball? No, but it does mean LeBron James should spend a lot of time on the court, because that's what he loves, that's what he's really good at, and that's what makes him feel fulfilled.

Hopefully, you can narrow things down a bit more. Maybe

Awesomeness Tip
"The hard part isn't figuring out what you are good at . . . it's having the courage to go for it, regardless of what any villain says to you!"—Josh Shipp

you've thought of four or five things you're really good at that you also enjoy. But maybe you're still not sure what your ultimate career will be or you're a little afraid to get started. That's completely understandable. We're just getting started, too. . . .

WORLD DOMINATION CHALLENGE

What dream or job would you try if you knew 100 percent there was absolutely no way you would ever fail? Write it down. Be specific!

// Just do it . . .

Here's what you do now: You start doing those things. Don't wait.

Sometimes we have a tendency to put off pursuing our goals until the absolute perfect time. There are so many things holding us back, after all. There's school, and soccer practice, and *Family Guy* is on at 7:30. Sometimes there's nothing going on, but you just don't feel like it. It's as if you have a magical fairy that comes down and pats your soft little head telling you, "It's OK . . . one day you'll be able to spend your time doing what you love. Don't worry about it right now. You can do it later. Maybe you should go back to playing Xbox."

Really, though, that magical fairy is a type of ghost. It's playing off the fears that have crept into your past by reminding you about the possibility of failure in your future. This fairy ghost is trying to keep you from doing what you love by reminding you how you might fail. She's hoping that you'll listen and put things off until it's too late. You need to grab that fairy by its frilly little fairy gown and punch it squarely in the mouth. You hear me? No more waiting. It's go time.

If you love playing video games, start learning all you can about how they're made. Learn who the big software companies are, and start thinking about what makes certain games epic and other games boring. Think about what sort of story lines work in a game, and what characters you like best. Start writing down game ideas in a notebook. Talk to your friends about games to find out what they like. Spend time reading game reviews and magazines. Do you want to be a game programmer? A writer? A critic? An animator? There are so many options you get to choose from!

If you love playing music, practice. Pick up those drumsticks or that guitar. Take music classes in school. Take private lessons. Pick up songs and albums from bands you like, then explore music Web sites or iTunes for bands you don't know so well. Play until your fingers bleed, not because you have to, but because you want to and nothing makes you feel more fulfilled.

Same goes for writing and math and cooking and sports and

law enforcement and whatever else. The more you practice your skills, the more involved you get, the better you become. Remember, too, that you're working toward a goal. Maybe you won't always like the bands you hear as you branch out, but you're listening to them because you want to be the best musician you can be, and it's research. The more you know about this skill, the better off you will be.

While you're working, pay attention to how you feel. Does playing guitar make you feel strong? Not like muscle strong, but emotionally and mentally strong? Could you play guitar for the rest of your life? If so, giddyap! If not, move on to a different skill. Don't spend the rest of your life playing guitar because you were afraid to try something different. That's not to say there won't be difficult days, even in your dream job. There will, trust me. But if you're not feeling strong anymore when you practice your skill, move on.

In the end, this is the only thing you can control. You can't make people love your music. You can't force people to watch you dance ballet. You can't force people to read your comic book or watch the movie you made. But you can work your butt off. And if you are that committed, I truly believe that you will get so good at your talent that you will have people showing up to listen, to watch, to read. You'll have people who can't help but love you.

Awesomeness Tip
"Even if you're on the right track, you'll get run over if you just sit there."—Will Rogers

// Finding friends in high places

Now that you're mastering your future career, it's time to address one of the best parts of dominating your career: Making friends (also see Chapter 17).

People (typically pirates) used to believe that everyone was on his or her own, that you reached the top only by outwitting, outplaying, and outlasting your opponents, all of whom are stranded on a desert island and split into two tribes with strange names, forced to compete in "challenges" for scarce resources, immunity, a million bucks, and the title of Sole Survivor. But that's not true. No one makes it on his or her own. We all need community around us to lift us up when we're down. We need others to help us.

Remember just a second ago when I said hard work is the only thing you can control? There is something else you can do that will help: Make friends who like the things you like. In your career, your allies are your greatest asset. Almost every great hero has allies, from Robin Hood to Rainbow Brite to Optimus Prime. Think of it like this: How many people do you know? How many people would you consider friends? Let's say the number is twenty. The thing is, those twenty people each have twenty friends who you don't know. So, in a sense, you're a friend of a friend of 400 people. That's math, not magic!

Of those 400 people, maybe there are a few who can find you opportunities in your career, but the odds get better the more people you know. It's not all about connections, though. And you definitely don't want to connect with someone only for the betterment of your career. That makes you a social climber, which is completely lame, and smells like ninjas and pirates. That means you are dominating someone else's world for your own benefit. You just broke Rule Number 2.

Now, it's easy to say go out and find a hundred friends, but how do you go about becoming friends with people who like what you like? You go out. Like music? Go to music venues or music shops. Like math? Go to math club. Get it? You could also go bowling or to a coffee shop or any number of things, but wherever you go, you'll meet people. We covered this more in Chapter 17.

// Help me, Obi-Wan Kenobi, you're my only hope . . .

Besides being characters in famous movies, what do Luke Skywalker, Darth Vader, the Karate Kid, and the X-Men have in common? The all had mentors. Luke had Obi-Wan Kenobi and Yoda. Darth Vader had Obi-Wan Kenobi and Yoda, too, but then he bailed on them for the Emperor (who falls under the category "wrong crowd"). The Karate Kid had Mr. Miyagi. The X-Men have Professor Xavier.

If you want to dominate your own career, you'll need a mentor, too.

If you want to be a rock star, though, you might have a hard time. It's not like Chris Martin and Pete Wentz are holding open auditions for protégés. That's OK. Mentors don't have to be rich or marry Ashlee Simpson. They need to be smart people you respect, who maybe know a thing or two about leading you in the right direction. As long as it's not a guy who lives in a van and wears a trench coat all summer, you're probably good.

You know how to get a mentor? Ask. That's all. Compared to everything else you have to do to dominate, it's fairly easy. Most people, if they aren't enormous jerks (or extremely busy), will be happy to help and guide you. At the very least, they can e-mail you some advice. All you need to do is find someone with similar skills to you who has some experience in the field.

Even if you don't know anyone who works in the career you want to pursue, there's this whole network of information that flies back and forth through a mystical field called "cyberspace." It's called the "Internet." So you go "online" and you "surf" your way to the right site. Let's say you're still trying to be a video-game designer. Find a video-game company you like, and send them an e-mail. All you have to say is, "My name is <YOUR NAME>. I want to become a video-game designer. Is there a video-game designer I can e-mail to get advice on following my dream?"

It's not like you even have to meet them. I mean, Stranger Danger still applies . . . but at least you can get insight from someone who's been there via e-mail or a phone call. If you're fortunate enough to know someone who works in your chosen career, ask them. There's a 97 percent chance they'll love to help. Maybe you can even shadow them around at their job.

// R-E-S-P-E-C-T

Considering that you could very well be entering a career field full of robots, you need to know what you are walking into. And to do that, we should look to a little espionage, or spying. Now, contrary to popular belief, the best spies aren't James Bond. They don't wear tuxedos, drive cars with machine guns hidden in the headlights, or shoot their way out of situations. The best spies understand the culture they are entering. They use the customs and languages of the other countries to get what they want. They use their ability to relate to their surroundings.

This means you need to understand the world around you. You need to listen and respect others. Kind of like a ninja, only with a heart of gold. So, more like a sneaky samurai. This is how you build connections and network with people who can help you. Even robots. The more you understand these villains, the easier it becomes to dodge their attacks. This is how you get a job. This is how you nail the interview.

Things like good handshakes (hint: good = firm), dressing nicely, and speaking clearly may seem old-fashioned. Really, though, they show confidence. If you're dressed well, it shows you care enough about the job to put on a nice shirt for once. If you speak clearly, others will understand and listen to you. If you make eye contact, it shows you're not afraid of the person you're speaking with. If you are reliable and come to an interview or meeting ten minutes early, it shows you are someone others can depend on. If you can do these things, your first impression is already taken care of. These seem like little things, but they're bigger than you think. Trust me on this.

Showing (and earning) respect isn't just about appearances and your grip, though. It also means listening—you know, paying attention to the other person. It means asking questions. If you're naturally outgoing, slow down . . . learn about the other person. If you're shy, that's OK, too, because then it's easy to sit and listen. This isn't about faking your way through life or manipulating people so they'll help you. It's about being genuinely interested in others. If you engage them and allow them to tell their stories, they will like you. If you respect them and treat them with kindness, they'll treat you the same way. Most of the time. But you know what? Even when they don't treat you well, your actions will not go unnoticed.

All these tips go double during job interviews. That's when you need to present yourself at your absolute best. Along with all those niceties and manners and fancy shirts and ties, it's important to be prepared. Think about the questions you're likely to face. Hiring managers like to ask about five-year plans and what you feel your biggest weakness is (here's a freebie: Do not mention laziness). The secret tip, though, is to do some research on where you're interviewing. Read up on what they do, how they work . . . anything you can possibly learn about the company. Then, when the manager asks, "Now, do you have any questions for us?" (they always do this, and it is a test to see how interested you are), you say, "Yes. I noticed in May of 2007, your company posted its highest quarterly profits. Would you say that was due to increased consumer confidence or to changes in the federal tax system, which subsequently subsidized wheat farming in Nebraska?"

Maybe that question isn't all that great. The point is, you've read up. You know what you're walking into (just like a spy). You know the culture, you know the history. You're one of them. You show that sort of thinking, and they'll love you for it.

// The two-year gap

"This is all well and good," you may be saying inside your mind, or maybe even outside your mind, to which passersby may react strangely. (That guy is talking to a book?)

But maybe you're just not there yet. Maybe you've shadowed a doctor through a day in the emergency room, and dealing with blood and guts is not for you. (This happened to me. Yeah, laugh it up—me and my crazy hair wanted to be a doctor.) Maybe you rode along with a cop, and while carrying a gun seemed cool, you weren't so into that uniform. Maybe you were the assistant to a traveling street magician for one day, and felt pulling quarters from kids' ears wasn't your thing. Maybe you've done all these things, and you're still not sure what you want to do. Maybe this happens the day after you graduate from high school or college. DO NOT PANIC. Your life is not over. You are not a failure. You just haven't found a dream to follow.

If that's the case, here's your ticket out. Take the two-year gap.

Here's how the two-year gap works. Make no financial

commitments. Don't buy a car or anything that's going to get you into debt. Drop your standard of living as far as it'll go. Instead of caviar and lobster, eat some Trader Joe's macaroni and cheese. (You know, the ones with the white Cheddar.) Then, use what funds you do have to do everything you can.

Wait tables. Go to art shows. Read books for fun and to learn a variety of stuff on your own terms. Intern at places that sound interesting. Travel! Hit the road for a bit and see what's out there. The goal here is input. Get input from everyone you can; ask to hear everyone's story. Absorb all this experience like a ShamWow sucking up a spill.

If, in two years, you still haven't found something that excites you, which makes you want to dive in, then . . . well, you might be on your own. But this is unlikely.

If you do find something—and I'm willing to put money on the fact that you will—start digging in. Try the whole job-shadow thing again, or read books on how to get there. If, after all this time, you find your real passion is being a garbageman (remember, great pay!), then it's time to learn how to make it happen.

// Good vs. great

Let's say it's a few years down the line. You've worked your way through an internship, and you're dancing and prancing your way into a profession that gives you real purpose. You've paid your dues, and you're riding along like a barnacle on the great *Titanic* of waste management (or rock stardom or video-game designerdom).

Maybe you've got a solid little flow of income, and you're thinking, "I'm doing what I love! Hooray!"

Well, you've accomplished more than what the world expected. You've become good. Above average. If you're working in a career you love, you're doing something a large chunk of the population will never realize. You deserve a milk shake for all your hard work, don't you! You deserve crumbled Oreos in that milk shake! While you're sitting there, sucking down your fancy, above-average milk shake, someone should hand you an award that says, GOOD JOB! YOU'RE ABOVE AVERAGE! You can read it while you slurp.

WRONG.

This is my number-one qualm with life. You know what above average is? You know what good is? I'll tell you. Let's say average is here (I'm putting my hand out in a line at about mouth level). Here's above average (I'm moving my hand up to my upper lip). Here's good (now my hand is right at the tip of my nose). This would've worked better if you could see me, because it's a really vivid visual tool. The point is, that's not good enough. I don't even care if you move up to eye level.

Never settle for above average. Never settle for good. A lot of people out there think good is enough, and maybe it is for them. It should not be enough for you. I don't want to sound like your overbearing ex-military father here, but the world needs greatness. Too many people settle for less.

There are going to be voices from inside and out. They'll tell you you're not good enough, or you're doomed to crumble. There will be voices that tell you to give up. They'll tell you to take the easy route. They'll tell you to settle.

Then, every so often, there will be a voice that says, "You're the best person in the world to do this. There is no one in the world better equipped. Not only can you do this, you can be the best. You can change the world . . . the people around you, your family . . . because this is what you were made to do."

And that voice, the one telling you to drive on because you'll own this . . . that voice is true. That's the voice to listen to.

> **Awesomeness Tip**
>
> "I've missed more than nine thousand shots in my career. I've lost almost three hundred games. Twenty-six times, I've been trusted to take the game-winning shot and missed. I've failed over and over and over again in my life. And that is why I succeed."
> —Michael Jordan

21.

How to Dominate
Your Goals

You know what I love? I love when a plan comes together. No matter what it is, whether it's planning the perfect date, planning a supercool weekend with friends, or planning out my goals for the year. I love it! Everything turns out so much better if you have a plan, yet remain flexible for a little spontaneity. It took me a long time to figure this out on my own, but once learned, the lesson changed my life.

If you don't believe me, answer me this: If you don't know where you're going, how will you ever know when you get there?

Red alert: That's a rhetorical question. The answer is: YOU WON'T.

And here's the thing:

// It's not enough to have a dream

I must point out a misconception about dreams. Heroes don't have dreams. Sleeping people have dreams. Are you sleeping right now? I didn't think so. (That was another rhetorical question—you gotta be quick with me.)

People who are awake have *goals*. Think about it, Martin Luther King might have had a dream about racial equality, but then he woke up and actually did something about it. I'm sure you have had a dream about doing something incredible or becoming someone awesome, but are you actually doing it? In other words—are you awake or sleeping?

// You need to have a plan

Any plan at all. It doesn't matter if it's as complicated as a Charles Dickens novel or as simple as a few points on a notepad or a Starbucks napkin. It doesn't matter if you've set goals for the next sixty years or just for the next three hours. Having a plan puts you a half step up. It gives you a framework, something to remember when you lose focus.

Start small. You don't need to know what career path you're going to follow, or where you're going to live, or whether you want a giant mansion in the suburbs or a cozy condo in a major city. Start with decisions you can make now.

MOST COMMON FORMS OF VILLAINY WITH GOALS
GHOSTS; ZOMBIES

Here's how to start: Write out a to-do list. Don't make it too difficult or in-depth. You can make your list a series of things you want to do. I'd suggest writing out three things MAX, stuff you can actually DO. If it's overwhelming and lengthy like an Old Testament scroll, you'll shut down, do nothing, and play Xbox all day. Trust me, I know.

Then, the next day when you wake up, look at your list. Ask yourself, "If I did only one thing on this list today, what would make me feel best? What would make me feel like today had been a good, productive day?"

Pick something—then accomplish that task before noon. Maybe it's writing a blog post on a new album you heard. Maybe it's studying for a history exam. Maybe it's asking out the girl in your math class who's been flirting with you via wordless glances. Whatever it is, make sure you get it done that day. Don't put it off.

You don't need to do everything on the list, just one thing. When you put your head on your pillow that night, you'll be able to think back on and say, "I got that done."

Awesomeness Tip
"He who fails to plan, plans to fail."
—Proverb

// It's all about making progress

I had a friend who wasn't happy with his weight, so he got a membership at a gym, and the gym provided a personal trainer. The first day, she worked him out until he puked.

The next day, his muscles were shredded and he couldn't lift his legs. He never went back to that gym.

He was still unhappy with his weight, though, so he joined another gym, a little farther away from his house. They gave him another personal trainer, but this dude took a different approach:

"I only want you to work out for fifteen minutes," the new trainer told him on his first day. "But you have to come back tomorrow."

"That's it?" my friend asked, eyeing him suspiciously, and the trainer nodded. My friend rode ten minutes on a stationary bike, then he lifted weights for five, and then he went home. The workout didn't kill him. He went back the next day.

"I'm glad to see you again," the trainer smiled. "This is your plan: You work out every day for as long as you like. It can be ten minutes or it can be two hours. All you have to do is show up and do something."

By the end of the year, my friend had lost a TON of weight. In fact, he got so fit, he finished the year by taking a 2,700-mile bike trip across the country. For fun.

Think about it: If my friend had started out by saying, "I want to be able to bike 2,700 miles," and just kept thinking about that bike trip every day, he would've felt constantly behind. He would've pushed his body to exhaustion, and at some point, he'd would've given up altogether. But just working out ten minutes a day . . . that's not so bad.

Point is: Little steps add up if you keep walking.

// Roll with the punches and kicks (and head butts)

The thing with a plan is, it's almost guaranteed *not* to work the way you want. Some guy named Murphy learned this, and he made it into his own law:

"Anything that can go wrong will go wrong." (Murphy sounds like king of the zombies, doesn't he?)

That's OK, though. That's how things work. You still need a plan.

The key is knowing things won't go flawlessly. There will be mountain-sized obstacles that rise up out of the ground. There will be hedgehog-sized obstacles, too.

Ultimately, you can't accomplish your plan by just writing it down. If your goal is to be an astronaut, you can't present a list of dreams scrawled in red crayon to the human-resources person at NASA and expect to be launched into space the next day (except maybe as a test subject—sucker).

If you have a plan and an obstacle suddenly blasts up in front of you, you can't sit there and cry. That's what babies do. Literally. They cry and wail until someone stuffs a binky in their mouth, and then they suckle their worries away.

Adaptation is crucial. Your mind-set, when that Mount Everest of conflict rises in front of you, should be to pause and think, "How do I get to the other side?" You can climb, or go around, or pay a Sherpa to helicopter you to the other side. Maybe you can find a more creative way around. The point is, you get around. You don't curl into a ball and sniffle, hoping the mountain will go away.

Conflict and adventure is what makes a great story. Which movie would you rather watch: *Star Wars,* or a film about how a whiny kid named Luke Skywalker lived and died working on a moisture farm on Tatooine? Sure, the latter might've been an interesting documentary about growing old doing boring stuff on a desolate sand planet, but it wouldn't have been *Star Wars.*

Set goals. Have a plan. Make progress. And, as you learn more about yourself and your strengths, it's okay to change your mind. But never, ever, just plain give up. That's no way to dominate your world!

22.

How to Dominate
Your Money

If you're not careful, your money will OWN you. Honestly, most of the developed world is a slave to money . . . and they think it's normal.

With money, as with nearly everything, you need to have a plan or you'll end up being dominated. You need to have goals. If you don't have a plan for your money, you are going to learn lessons the hard way. If you don't have a plan, it will usually end in boredom, epic failure, or jail. How can I write a line like that without backing it up with a story?

// Storytime with Josh

When I was a young lad of eighteen, someone gave me a check-
book. Sweet! Free money, right? So I started writing checks for all
different sorts of things. I could finally buy the clothes and music
and DVDs that I'd been wanting but was too lazy to work and
earn the money for! Before my screwed-up money situation came
to a crashing halt, I actually ended up writing over $10,000 worth
of bad checks! As I'm driving along one day rocking to some music (that I probably paid for with a bad check), I get pulled over by
a cop. I was going 70 in a 55-mile-per-hour zone, so I figured I was
getting a ticket for at least $200, which was a lot more cash than I
had in my empty checking account at the time. Even worse was
the matter of my car insurance because, well, I wasn't sure I really
had any, since I'd been sending in bad checks to pay for it. And
in Oklahoma, driving without insurance is a criminal offense. I
prayed that maybe the nice state trooper wouldn't notice. . . .

"Young man, I need you to step out. You've got a problem
bigger than a speeding ticket."

He brought me to the back of the patrol car and told me to put
my hands on the trunk. He then took my wrists, one at a time,
pulled them behind my back, and slid steel handcuffs on me.

Next stop: Jail.

That's right, folks. I was a jailbird, a criminal, a felon, a convict,
an outlaw, a delinquent . . . you get the point. And you know whose
fault that was? Mine. I can't blame anyone else for it. I can't blame

the fact that no one went out of their way to pull me aside and teach me about money. I can't blame the school system for not teaching us about checkbooks or how ATMs are not magical money machines (who knew?). I can't blame my parents for leaving me at the hospital so they could avoid the responsibility of teaching me everything I needed to know about money. The only person to blame is me. I never made a plan for myself, so I ended up learning the hard way.

After a night in jail swapping stories with Cyclone (a hardened convict/tattoo artist who gave me my first tattoo—of a fire truck—on my forehead), I knew I had to make some changes in my life. I'm kidding about the tattoo, by the way. But that night in jail shook me up. I needed to develop a financial plan and I needed to get out of debt.

Have you ever gotten in trouble for your money habits? It's most likely because you never actually developed a plan to guide your spending. Maybe it's too late and you've already made bad financial decisions. Are your money-ghosts haunting you? They definitely haunted me, but I finally found a way to overcome them. I'm here to help so YOU don't have to learn the hard way. No more excuses. I'm here to share with you my financial plan, which I use today, as well as some wise words I wish someone would have told me when I was a young buck.

// Money can make you happy!!

Have you ever heard the phrase "Money can't make you happy"? Well, it's a full-on lie! I have found one way that money can actually make you superhappy—guaranteed. How?

By giving money away.

"Josh, you want me to give away my money? Are you crazy?!" you may be thinking. Yes, I most likely am crazy . . . but stick with me.

My scientists at the Hey Josh Institute of Knowledge informed me that by their calculations, the average teenager has just under $20 on them at any given time. Maybe you don't have it on you right now, but you've probably got about that much if you add up all your loose change.

Do me a favor. Draw a circle and write "the world" below it. Now, draw a line through the circle, cutting it in half. In one half, write "$2." Why? Because half of the world lives on just about two dollars a day. That's right. Two bucks. Let that sink in for a second.

I want you to understand this. You are filthy, stinkin', crazy, unbelievably rich. You might not feel like it because everyone keeps telling you that you need more money, but you are rich! Just think about how easy it is for you to spend $2, the same amount half of the world lives on each day. What did you buy today that cost two dollars? A Coke? A TV show on iTunes? A Jr. Bacon Cheeseburger at Wendy's? Potato chips? It's easier to spend $2 than it is to think of anything that costs *less* than $2.

"OK, that's great, I've got a little cash. But it's MY money, why would I give it away?" Yes, it is your money. Yes, you earned it. Yes, you can do whatever you want with it.

But let's take a tour of crazy town together. Ready?

The world is full of villains who want to get their hands on as much money as they can. Ninjas want to trick others into giving it to them. Robots are programmed to work, work, work to make as much money as possible. They think they can actually dominate the world if they have enough cash. In fact, they spend hours and hours each day wondering how they can make more and spend less, how they can sell more products, and pay employees less. When you consider how much people stress about getting more and more money, it's almost like they've become a slave to it.

I'm not down with being a slave to anything. Are you?

So, gut check:

// Who's dominating what here?

Do you actually dominate your own world when it comes to money? Or does the world's money mentality dominate you? If you physically cannot give away any of your money, I hate to tell you this, but you are a slave to money. I don't care if you think this doesn't apply to you because you don't have much money. It's not about an amount, but a mind-set. Get rid of your "slave-to-money" mind-set and get free! Give away some of your money! Right now! If you can't bring yourself to do it, it's time to get honest with yourself and ask, Why not?

Want money to make you happy? Find something you really really care about and throw your money at it!

Maybe someone in your family died of cancer and you want to help find a cure—GIVE!

Maybe you want to provide a shot that will keep a child in Africa from getting malaria from a tiny mosquito—GIVE!

Maybe you want to purchase a goat for a village that will give a family milk for years to come—GIVE!

I'm sure you're creative when it comes to spending money. Now get creative when it comes to giving it away.

You can't dominate the whole world. You can't dominate how others spend. But you DO have control over your own life and how you spend your own money. I hope that when you choose to dominate your own world, it's a beautiful world with no slavery to money. I hope it's a world of complete freedom where you can open your eyes, see a need, and do something about it.

// Debt hates your sweet grandmother

Hold your breath: If you haven't received it already, you will very soon—a white envelope addressed to you, saying you are special. In fact, you are so special that you are "preapproved" to open a credit-card account!!

That letter seems completely harmless, almost exciting, doesn't it? It even makes you feel a little bit important, like an adult. But what does that letter really mean? It means this ninja credit-card company has determined that you are a preapproved sucker. They know that you are young and might not know much about creating a financial plan, and are hoping that you allow villains to dominate your world. They are counting on the fact that your desire to be accepted and "preapproved" by the world will cause you to sign up for this little plastic ninja membership card.

You want approval? Well, guess what . . . since you are reading this book then I, Josh Shipp, preapprove you.

> I preapprove you to throw that letter in the trash without even opening it.
>
> I preapprove you to shred the crap out of the envelope with your parent's lawn mower.
>
> I preapprove you to chuck it in a roaring fire and spit upon its shriveling paper.
>
> I preapprove you to take control of your own life and quit letting some ninja corporate executive in a suit sitting on the fifty-eighth floor of a skyscraper in New York City dominate your world and take your money.
>
> I preapprove you to live a life of freedom, not a life where your decisions are made by your debt.

You know about Debt, right? No, it's not even worthy of capitalization. It shall be hereafter known as debt because it's such a sneaky ninja. For crying out loud, it even has a silent "b" in the word! There's only four letters, yet one of them is silent!? Seriously! NINJA ALERT!!!

If you're not familiar with debt, let me introduce you . . .

> debt loves to put you in tough situations.
>
> debt stresses you out by taking away your options.
>
> debt gives you wedgies that require special medical attention.

debt sends you spam e-mail about words that I don't even want
to say.

debt causes arguments between your parents.

debt kicks your kitten in the face.

debt makes out with your boyfriend while you volunteer at the
nursing home.

debt constantly tells really lame "your mom" jokes.

debt clubs baby seals.

debt spits in your food when you go through the drive-through.

debt says you throw like a sissy.

debt denies your friend request on Facebook! And let's be honest,
that's low—no one denies friend requests on Facebook.

debt hates your sweet, sweet grandmother.

debt offers you a lot, but actually takes from you. debt is what happens when you buy things you don't need, with money you don't have, to impress people you don't even know. How on earth does that fit in with dominating your own world?! It doesn't.

Let me explain. If you use your credit card to buy $100 worth of clothes in one month, that means you are borrowing $100 from the credit card company. Then they only ask you to pay them back $25 per month since they are "such nice people" (classic ninja tactic).

Sounds great, right? But remember, you still owe them $75. Since they did you this "wonderful" favor of delaying your payments, they're going to charge you a little tiny fee of about $15 bucks. Now, that $75 you owe them has become $90.

Congratulations! You are now in debt. Welcome to the "Pre-approved Sucker Club." And here's what membership looks like (warning, it could make you cry like a twelve-year-old at a Jonas Brothers concert):

- The average eighteen-year-old's debt = $3,300
- Average credit card debt = $8,500
- Average student loan debt = $19,400
- Average household debt = $38,000
- Average twenty-eight-year-old's debt = $66,000

Stings, doesn't it? My advice to you: Don't become another statistic.

Sure, at first, that $15 a month seems like nothing, but as you can see above, debt slowly continues to creep up on you, becoming bigger and bigger, eventually turning into thousands of dollars while you flash your shiny credit card. I understand that you want to go out to eat with your friends all the time. However, the financial cost of all those little fried chicken fingers will stay with you for years and years to come. At least you had those few seconds of salty goodness, though! I hope you're happy.

High school is just the beginning of this madness. After high school, credit-card companies attack you at college. When you show up, they try to trick you with XXL T-shirts, stress balls, or stupid pens that don't even work in exchange for your card application. These ninjas offer you crap products, then take your money! Be careful, the really smart ninja credit-card companies will offer you iPods or cash or whatever the newest coolest tool is.

See their strategy? These ninjas are trying to grab you the second you leave your parents' side, when you're scared of being alone and you're establishing your independence. You start looking around at the other students with their cool clothes, backpacks, and laptops, and you think you need the same stuff. debt loves the vampire trap. debt wants you to become a vampire as soon as possible, and debt will front the cash! It's like a ninja/vampire combo attack. (I hate it when villains combine forces!)

But you are too smart to fall for any of this ninja foolishness. You know that cool isn't for sale. If you are going to dominate your world, you don't want some ninja company telling you how to spend your money, do you? Let us recall Rule Number 1: No person (or company) has the right to dominate your world. That's *your* job, hero.

> **Awesomeness Tip**
> "Never spend your money before you have it."—Thomas Jefferson (Seriously, why wouldn't you listen to T. J.? He was smart enough to actually be printed on money.)

// Cool isn't for sale

This is probably the hardest thing you will ever have to comprehend when it comes to money. And to be honest with you, I know that I still struggle with this even today. I still find myself attracted to some things (a car, shoes, speakers, etc.) someone else has that I don't. But then I have to remind myself. I am Josh Shipp. I am defined by who I am. I am not defined by what I have or the things I buy (see: Identity).

Let us take a step back and start at the beginning of cool. What is cool? I think "cool" is an idea of elitism that a specific group creates and accepts for themselves. But who decides what becomes the new "cool" thing?

Vampires. Vampires created the idea of cool to dominate your world. No surprise there. Because vampires are typically über-popular, mysterious, charming, and intriguing, we occasionally get the urge to imitate them. But because they dress or act a certain way that feels out of our league, you feel like you don't really fit in with them. So you start buying the same clothes the vampires have, listening to their same music, going to the same spots they hang out at. Think about it. Rock stars ALWAYS create clothing trends that we all look up to. Models ALWAYS tell you which body image is most attractive to guys. The quarterback is ALWAYS at the coolest parties, and the head of the cheerleading squad is ALWAYS at the center of attention of the school's fashion scene. If you can keep up with their guidelines for being cool, then you've succeeded; you're cool. You are just like them. Until they decide what the next cool thing is.

When vampires control what is "cool," they control you and dominate your world.

So, what does this have to do with money? *There is a huge temptation for people to buy cool.* You try to buy the rock star's look. You wear the right clothes or say the right words to get invited to the quarterback's party. You blow three weeks' allowance on a bottle of diet pills that somehow fail to endow you with Gisele Bündchen's measurements.

I remember wanting one pair of shoes so bad because they

would make me look cool, and I would be accepted. I ended up throwing them in the garbage one year later. Why? Because there was already a new pair of cool shoes. However, I had spent so much money on last year's model I couldn't afford these new ones. Keeping up with cool never stops. It's like trying to reach the finish line when you're running on a treadmill. When you get older, it's about eating at the right restaurants, driving the right car, or having the perfect suit.

But "cool" changes drastically between age groups, geographic locations, and cultures. When Henry VIII was king, it was super-cool to be fat and pale. If you live in some areas of Africa, it's cool to have a ton of metal rings around your neck. There is no one, solid, universal definition of what is cool. Cool is relative. That means throughout your life, you will be associating yourself with many different groups, each with its own definition of cool. Right now it might be high school, but then comes college. Then you discover what is cool at your workplace or church or country club. Then you'll compare cool with a bunch of senior citizens at your nursing home. Then when you die, your family will talk with the funeral-home director and ask which coffin is the coolest to be buried in. See my point? Since cool is always changing and evolving depending on where you are at in life, you are left with two options:

Option 1: Try to always be cool. This means you need to devote tons of time to sniffing out upcoming trends. You also need plenty of money to pay for an endless succession of new things. You also will need to be able to ditch your current friends quickly. For example, if being cool becomes smoking weed, you'll need to get rid of your old friends who don't want to liquidate brain cells. You should also be aware that your car is of utmost importance, because you need to get out to all the cool parties. The worst part is, the older you get, the more money people are making, which means it's even harder to keep up with the coolest stuff. You think sneakers are bad; do you have any idea how much the finest Italian loafers run?

I'll be honest with you. I've tried to do this before. It's expensive and it's exhausting. The treadmill analogy is more accurate than you think. In fact, even when I was doing all the right things, I felt lonely. There was always another person who had a cooler car, or dressed better. I finally had to realize those people telling me what was cool (the vampires) were dominating my world. I had to stop. There had to be a better way. Which brings me to Option 2.

Option 2: Be you. Buy clothes that make you feel good about yourself, not what others want you to wear. Do the activities and wear the clothes that line up with your view of dominating your world, not a vampire's view. Once you eliminate all this scrambling to stay cool, you can focus your time on doing exactly what you want to do with your life, not what is required of you to pay the mounting credit-card bills. This is what it looks like to dominate your own world: Living for what you want to live for, not what everyone expects you to be, say, or do.

A house is where you live, a car gets you to and from where you need to go, and clothes keep you from being naked in public.

You don't need the most expensive versions of these things to be happy or cool. When the vampires can't control you any longer, they can't dominate your world. You've succeeded in the most important role of your life, being you.

WORLD DOMINATION CHALLENGE

But what about you? Are you impressed with people who have the fancy clothes or the fastest car? If so, why do you think that is? Do you think they are better, smarter, or cooler than you?

23.

How to Dominate
Your Body

I t's easy to dominate your body. Here's the formula: Work out for three hours every day. Take steroids. Skip meals. Pay bajillions of dollars to have plastic surgery.

NO. Don't. Those are the lies of the ninjas and vampires.

Just like they try to control you by defining what is cool, the villains of the world will try to enslave you to gym memberships, tanning salons, and beauty regimens by telling you how you should look.

Don't let them. Just as with money, you have a choice here: (a) let the vampires tell you how to look; or (b) be you.

I'll let you decide.

That said, it's important to . . .

// Treat yourself right

Contrary to popular metaphors, our bodies do not work the same as cars. With a new car, you take it off the lot, and it's ready to go. It's powerful, the steering is tight, and it has that distinct scent associated with buyer's guilt. Mmm, chemicals.

It's all downhill from there. Over time, your car piles on the miles, the spark plugs get less sparky, the oil gets black with sludge, and the cracks between the seats hide receipts, dropped pens, and the occasional French fry (don't worry . . . they have too many preservatives to rot).

The human body, on the other hand, takes around twenty years to reach its peak.

From that point forward, it's up to you whether you want to be driving when you're forty in: (a) a cherried-out classic Mustang convertible; or (b) a broken-down rusted Hyundai without hubcaps or a muffler.

We all, based on our personalities, have our weaknesses when it comes to physical health, and we all, to some extent, have addictive personalities, whether it's junk food, alcohol, nicotine, television, sex, or other things. Anything that makes us feel good or boosts our self-image can slip into a dangerous lifestyle choice. Even fitness can be an addiction.

Maintaining moderation in all things is much harder than it seems. Often, it's not enough to trust your willpower. The earlier you can remove the temptation of unhealthy lifestyles, the easier they are to cope with, so separating yourself from situations where you may slip is the first line of defense.

> ## MOST COMMON FORMS OF VILLAINY IN HEALTH
> ### NINJAS; VAMPIRES

// Avoid addiction

My friend Stephen smoked for eight years. He knew he was damaging his body. He didn't have as much energy as he used to, his breath was bad, and—this is kind of graphic—he'd cough up chunks of green phlegm every morning, hacking them into the bathroom sink. (Warned you.)

It wasn't that he didn't like smoking. He loved smoking. He thought it was cool. You're holding fire in your hands. You're breathing smoke. It curls out of your mouth like you're a dragon. Humphrey Bogart smoked. With a cigarette, you can gesture with your hands and it seems like you're more important. Stephen always had an excuse to take breaks during work, and no one cared.

Despite all that, Stephen knew he was killing himself. Every day that he was still smoking was one more day he didn't feel right. To quit, Stephen got a prescription for recently developed smoking cessation drug.

You're supposed to take this drug twice a day for three months. Right away, though, Stephen could feel the effects. His need for nicotine was gone. Stephen smoked a few cigarettes for the first week, but the desire went away, and he went twenty days without smoking. He felt free—felt better than he had in years—and was sure he had quit. He stopped taking the this drug after two weeks.

But the reason you're supposed to take the drug for ninety days, even though the physical addiction is gone in the first week or so, is to learn to live a life without cigarettes.

Soon Stephen was smoking his favorite cigarette of the day: The one with his morning coffee. Two weeks later, he was smoking if he was out with friends. Then he was smoking after every meal. Pretty soon, he was back to his previous habit.

He's stopped now. He got another prescription for the exact same drug, paid the couple of hundred dollars a second time, and went through the full ninety days.

The point is, addiction is rarely *just* physical. It is usually a mental crutch—a brain vampire chained to a ghost—meant to help us get through a situation. Maybe we have a few drinks at a party to loosen up, maybe we need an energy drink to get us going in the morning, maybe a cigarette helps us to take a time-out from a hectic schedule. All addictions start out in increments—one tiny little bit at a time. The only way to remain addiction-free is to avoid those vices altogether.

Of course, sometimes that's not possible. And most of the time, there's nothing wrong with a glass of wine (if you're of legal drinking age, of course!) or a cup of coffee every now and then. In fact, those things can be very enjoyable. It's when they become necessary to your everyday life that things go downhill. Even worse, you start to enjoy them less and less. Stephen's first cigarette in the morning with a steaming cup of black coffee was a pleasure. But paying $5 per day and interrupting his schedule every hour or so with a need for a bit-ter breath of burning tobacco out in the rain was not.

// Stay active

Because of our growing dependence on technology, most of us lead very sedentary lives. That's a fancy way of saying we spend most of our time on our butts. We sit at computers all day at work, then go home and spend our time in front of the television, or on the Internet, or playing video games. Some estimates claim between 20 and 30 percent of Americans are obese. Not a few pounds over-weight, not big-boned, not husky, but obese.

I think the biggest issue is a lack of exercise. Lying around becomes an addiction, too. Our bodies are built for physical activity, and many of us have lost the sense of what our bodies can do.

My friend Sarah was a songwriter, but she was short on cash. She applied as a barista at a major coffee chain. The first day she worked four hours, all on her feet. By the end of the day she could hardly stand. She went home that night and laid in the bathtub. Her feet were swollen and weary, and her back was unbearably tight. She couldn't imagine going back the next day.

But she did.

Three days later, she could stand for hours with hardly a break. She was amazed at how her body dealt with the changes.

It's like that in almost everything. If you go backpacking up in the mountains, you'll want to die within the first few hours.

Three days in, you're ready to march ten miles with forty pounds on your back.

I heard a story once about a man who was unhappy with his life. He was in his forties, and his life was falling apart. He hated his job, and he was fought with his wife and teenage daughter constantly. He was overweight and tired all the time, and life was a massive disappointment.

So he decided to kill himself.

But if he just offed himself with a gun or jumped off a bridge or something, his life insurance wouldn't pay out. His family would lose their house and savings, and his daughter would never get into school.

So, he devised a plan to have a heart attack. For two months, he ate the worst foods he could imagine. He shoveled down doughnuts and cupcakes at work. He ate massive helpings of steak and buttered bread for dinner. At lunch, he bought fast food—supersized—and forced himself to swallow it all. Instead of water, he drank soda and booze. The only thing he didn't shove down his gaping maw were vegetables. He even tried to take up smoking, but couldn't handle it more than a few days.

Then, after the two months, he went out for a run.

A long one. Miles and miles. Almost a marathon. He decided to run until his heart collapsed from the effort.

A quarter mile in, he was panting and heaving. At a half mile, sweat was spurting from his pores and his clothes were soaked. At a mile, he knew he was close. He was afraid of death, but he knew he couldn't turn back. He thought about how awful his life was, and he ran on. For six miles he ran on.

But he never collapsed. After the sixth mile, his muscles were exhausted, and he could run no farther. His heart was beating out of his chest, but it didn't stop.

Then, a weird thing happened. He felt really, really good. "Maybe this is the euphoria before death," he thought. But it wasn't. He decided to try again the next day.

The next day, despite every muscle in his body shrieking in pain, he ran again. This time, he made it seven miles before his legs gave out, but his heart kept beating. Strangely, he felt good again.

He kept trying for a week, and it never worked. He got faster and faster, and could run farther each time, but his heart wouldn't die. He felt better and kept running. The weight fell away, and he started to eat healthier because it made him feel even better. He gained his energy back and was in a better mood. He became more patient with his family, and began to think maybe he should try a new career path—maybe get a job he'd be more happy with.

Sometimes we like to pretend it's not there, but there's a link between our body and our spirit in our mind. One part of us can't be fully healthy without the other. Similarly, if we focus too much on our physical selves, our head and heart won't be working at their full potential.

Not all of us are athletes, so it's important to find physical activities we enjoy, whether it's team sports or individual, competition against ourselves or others. There are plenty of opportunities out there, so just try one out. If softball or basketball aren't your thing, try Frisbee, golf, skateboarding, biking, or hiking through a nature preserve.

The point is, you can't dominate your world without controlling your physical body.

24.

How to Be a Communication Hero

There's a good chance if you're reading this book that you are a member of either Generation Y (born between the early '80s and mid-'90s) or the millennial generation. I'm a superearly Gen-Y baby myself.

If you are, you've been raised in a world of limitless communication. I'm going to get all old man on you for a second: When I was a youngster, long distance was expensive, mobile phones were in their infancy (and the size of a suitcase), and only a select few computer nerds where dreaming about the possibility of electronic mail ("we'll call it 'e-mail' for short!" they decided). The easiest form of communication was still a stamped letter carried by horse and buggy to its final destination. Just kidding. But it's true that letters were pretty much the speediest way to communicate. Or a fax machine. Man, those were lame!

These days we are connected nearly all of the time. We can have relationships with people all over the world. I can talk to almost any of my friends face-to-face while I write these words, sitting in a hotel lobby in San Jose. To us, this is just an everyday reality, but if you take a moment to think about it, it's mind-boggling.

There are upsides and downsides to the advent of the Internet. Communication is one of the upsides.

Still, it pays to run through a quick course on communicating at all levels. No matter how connected we are, we still need to communicate with people face-to-face, so let's start there.

// Even though you're five feet away, I'd feel better if we texted

I don't care if you're the greatest e-mailer on the wide, green planet Earth. You could still suck at meeting someone face-to-face.

Ask any poker professional: The majority of our F2F communication is not in the words we say; it's in how we say them. Our inflection, tone, and body language convey our true meaning.

Compare and reflect:

Scenario A: "How are you today?" the starting linebacker asked little freshman Sammy Jackson in the hall after first period. He extended his hand and smiled wide. "Welcome to Lincoln High School!"

Scenario B: "How are you today?" the starting linebacker asked little Sammy Jackson in the hall after period, right before he punched Sammy in the stomach, sending the freshman's books spinning across the polished floor. As he walked away to the laughter of his teammates, he shouted over his shoulder, "Welcome to Lincoln High School!"

You get the point. Same words, different meaning.

If we mumble, slouch, and dart our eyes toward the ground, we convey, at best, discomfort with the situation. At worst, we look like guilty criminals. While it's true that we shouldn't judge a book by its cover, a bad first impression can be devastating, especially if we want to make an ally.

When you meet someone for the first time, follow these four tips:

Stand up straight. By using good posture, you let people know you are confident and strong, and they will admire that.

Use a firm handshake. You don't need to squeeze like Lenny from *Of Mice and Men*. Just a firm grip. A weak handshake feels weird, and gives the sense you don't really care about talking to this person. You'd be surprised how few people understand this basic principle. If you're a woman, a firm handshake isn't as necessary, but it's still a good idea. You don't want your hand to feel like a clam. No one likes touching a clam. Seriously, I got goose bumps (the bad kind) just thinking about it. If you're a guy, and you shake hands with a girl who has a stronger grip than you, you can pretty much count her out as a prospective date.

Maintain eye contact. Look the person in the eye, and maintain that eye contact when you're speaking to him or her. Like

handshakes, you want to do this within reason. If you stare at someone wide-eyed and unblinking for minutes on end, they might get
creeped out.

Speak clearly, and with confidence. Don't worry. No one has a
complete mastery of the English language. But you're definitely
not going to be heard if you mumble one decibel above a whisper
and slur your words together. You don't
need to use fancy words in an attempt to
sound smart. The goal is simple communication, not a word-of-the-day calendar
expo.

> *Awesomeness Tip*
> "It's not what you say; it's how you say it."   —Josh Shipp

// What did you say?

You know how I say, "It's not what you say; it's how you say it"?
Well, there's a catch. If you're saying things like, "I wish you were
dead," or "Your mamma's so fat," or otherwise making threats or
rude jokes, or tearing people down . . . it's DEFINITELY what you're
saying that matters.

Your tongue is one of the toughest parts of your body to control. Unfortunately, there's no getting words back; once you've set
'em free in the world, they're out there for good, lodged in someone's memory, where they'll stay potentially forever. They may come
back to haunt you. They may come back to haunt the one who
heard them. Either way, such words are better left unsaid. You don't
want to be responsible for creating ghosts.

If you have a hard time figuring out what to say and what not to say, try a little exercise I like to call "Word Math." I'm not talking about those tricky SAT questions where they ask you about where and what time two trains meet if one train leaves from Chicago at 1 P.M. traveling toward Boston at 70 mph and the other train leaves Boston at 3 P.M. traveling toward Chicago at 56 kph (just to be tricky). I hate those problems. They make my eyeballs numb. No, Word Math is simple. Basically, everything you say is either going to add to someone or subtract from them. If it subtracts from them—tears them down or makes them feel stupid or otherwise hurts their feelings—it's probably not a nice thing to say. And you should either not say it at all or, if it's too late, apologize, and quickly. If it adds to other people and makes them feel better and encourages them or makes them laugh, you're probably OK.

Another note: Know your audience. This is key. Remember those listening skills I've been telling you are so important? Bust 'em out here. If you want to get through to people, speak their language. Try not to offend them. Use words and illustrations they can relate to. Your grandpa probably doesn't have a clue about the "Internets" and may just be learning how to operate one of those flashy new VCR thingamajiggers; telling him you "Googled" something is just gonna confuse him.

// The call is coming from inside the house

Mastery of phone communication has nothing to do with the person you're calling or the person calling you. The first step is being courteous to the people you're around.

Unless you're discussing national security policy, no one else wants to hear your one-sided conversation (and even then, only Russian spies would care). If you're in a movie theater, the grocery line, or any other place where others are stuck standing next to you while you prattle on about last night's Lakers game or how you can't BELIEVE what she said about so-and-so, take it somewhere else. Find a place where people don't have to listen to you. Otherwise, you come off like an enormous tool.

The same goes for plenty of other activities. If you're operating heavy machinery—particularly something that requires a large amount of focus (like driving a car or Mack truck)—get off the phone. You are not as good at multitasking as you think you are. That's nothing to be ashamed of . . . no one is. They've done studies.

Of course, there are situations where you need to take a call when you're driving. If you do (and it's legal in your state), make it short or have a passenger do the talking.

Otherwise, the rules are the same. Speak clearly, and loud enough to be heard.

// OMG! LOL!

As awesome as electronic communication is, its unique immediacy and absence of body language also make it easy to mess up.

Problem 1: Inflection and meaning can be lost. While this issue improves as people learn how to effectively communicate through writing, it still requires a deft writing hand to communicate not only the message, but the tone. If you're using all capital letters, and a 747 full of exclamation points, you'll give the impression that you're always yelling, and no one likes a yeller.

Problem 2: We don't have time to dwell on what we say. You know how when your temper flares up, you're supposed to count to ten and cool down? With the instant gratification of e-mail, text messages, and Twitter, we can reply in seconds, often without considering the other person's view, and often slathered in a healthy poutine of emotion, good and bad.

Problem 3: Sarcasm doesn't translate well into writing. 'Nuff said.

Remember the scene in *Anchorman* where the rival news teams meet up in an empty industrial complex, and it quickly turns into an epic battle?

E-mail conversations, message-board threads, and online chats have a tendency, like the *Anchorman* battle, to get out of hand quickly. The reason is, all we have to do is type and send, and it takes thirty seconds (if you're slow). One minute you're peacefully discussing plans for the evening, and the next thing you know your best friend is threatening to rob you in your sleep.

It's so tempting, when we've finished composing a nasty witty response to a real or imagined slight to click that Send button. In reality, maybe we're best off waiting a day or two before replying. Almost every time I've waited to send a hot-tempered e-mail I've written, I've found a better, more civil way to voice my position in the morning. I've probably spared myself quite a bit of heartache that way.

Problem 4: Professionalism. There's nothing wrong with informality among friends, but we need to remember not everyone knows us or reads our e-mails the same way. Your boss may not understand your sarcastic sense of humor (see Problem 3 above). The girl you're interested in may not be amused by videos of Chinese bike riders crashing into four-foot-deep puddles in the sidewalk. In all electronic exchanges, it's crucial to really think about who we're communicating with, and to err on the side of caution.

// All apologies

While we're on the subject of communication, I want to say something about apologies.

When communication begins to break down, it's like a bomb that needs defusing, like in an episode of 24. The quickest way to defuse a situation is to apologize.

It may not be your fault completely, but every conflict—every miscommunication—involves mistakes on both sides. I guarantee, nothing will defuse that bomb quicker than owning up to your mistakes.

Take a moment to look at what went wrong, then apologize for your part. Maybe your part is small, or maybe it's big, but an apology will immediately help reduce tension and lower defenses.

Apologize authentically.

"I'm sorry you reacted that way to what I said about your <blank>," is not an apology. You cannot apologize for how someone else reacts. You can only apologize for your actions.

If you're not sorry, don't apologize, but there's a 99.83 percent chance you DO have something to apologize for. It's your job to find what that something is, own up to it, and make amends.

You may not see the results immediately, but I promise you'll be better off in the long run. It goes against every fiber of our being to admit our weakness and surrender to someone else . . . but that may be why it works so effectively.

// "You're such a great listener!"

As always, communication also comes down to listening.

"But, Josh," you may be crying, "I suck at listening!"

Yeah, listening isn't always that easy, so here's a tip therapists use: Mirroring. Basically, mirroring means repeating back what someone has said. In couples therapy, you're supposed to repeat your partner's words, almost like you're imitating them. If you do that in real life, people might think you were raised on a different planet, so you'll have to tone it down some and just repeat back main points.

This works particularly well against robots. Here's an example from a conversation with your school counselor, Counsel-bot 2000:

> **Counsel-bot 2000:** *Your grades are not good enough. If you do not improve your GPA, your top university choice will not accept you.*
>
> **You:** *So, are you saying I'm not going to get into my top choice?*

Counsel-bot 2000: No! I am sorry. I seem to have
miscommunicated. What I am saying is that if you bring
your GPA up a few points, you can make it in.
You: That's good to hear. Let's talk about how I can bring
my GPA up . . .

On the surface, it may seem like the school counselor doesn't
believe in you, and doesn't think you can meet the requirements
to get into the college of your choice. If you take a step back and
look at it from your counselor's perspective, or ask your counselor
to clarify, you'll see she is merely encouraging you to improve your
grades, and is actually looking out for you.

Of course, if you're like me and the ADD kicks in, you might
fade out after a few sentences.

I realize how ridiculous this sounds, but I'm telling you, it works.
If you're actively listening, you're not busy building up your defense
in your mind as soon as your boyfriend starts talking. It forces you
to put yourself in the other person's shoes, and to see that the other
person isn't attacking you.

The best communicators understand the importance of listening. Think about it: How good would my expert advice be if I didn't
read the actual question?

25.

How to Be a Hero with Your Talents

Before we get started, a word of warning:

// Don't get cocky

Odds are, you have some pretty mad skills. Maybe you can triple jump like a jackrabbit, make your own clothes, or tell jokes so funny that Granny has a heart attack. That's great (although try to hold back a little around Granny; she's delicate).

But here's the thing: No matter how good you are, you'll almost always find someone better than you. And since you're just not cut out to be awesome at everything, there will be areas where you're really quite bad. Like me: I can run a marathon, but I can't tell my left from my right. Pretty embarrassing sometimes.

My point is, if you look around, you'll always be able to find people that you're faster than, stronger than, hotter than, and just plain better than at various tasks, games, skills, or whatever. By the same token, you'll ALWAYS be able to find people that are more attractive or more talented than you. Sorry, but it's true.

But guess what?

// Comparing yourself doesn't matter

You are NOT BETTER than other people, and they're NOT BETTER than you.

You are you, and they are them. Simple as that. You're not going to establish your identity by comparing yourself to other people. Any time you find yourself comparing yourself to others, STOP, drop, and roll—you may not know it, but you're labeling them in a small way. Truly being yourself is not about being better or worse than others. It's about being YOUR best.

Remember that and you'll be able to pull the fangs out of every vampire that comes along. You'll be able to dismantle robot machinery and stop zombies dead (er, undead? re-dead?) in their tracks. And you'll resist the urge to become a vampire yourself. Instead, you'll be able to flex your talents and abilities with controlled, humble confidence.

So, as we already know . . .

// "The Dream" is to make a living doing something we love

But, as I previously mentioned, making a living doing something we love takes a lot of practice, a pile of effort, and a heaping table-spoon of luck.

Let's be honest here: Not all of us have the time and income to spend all day, every day, following our muse. There are bills and dues to pay now, homework to turn in, and dishes to wash after dinner. The vast majority of us don't get offered our dream job out of nowhere, or have an overflowing trust fund, which gets us out of work.

It's not just about following your dreams, though. Even if you reach the top of your dream field, even if you've completely domi-nated your career and you're getting paid billions of dollars to do what you would do for free, you should still have interests outside of that area.

My friend Sonny is a movie director, and a pretty successful one. He's doing the job he's always dreamed of. But he can't do it all the time, or he'd be a smoldering wreck of a man, so he balances his job with his hobbies. He cooks, and plays video games, and spends time with the people he cares about. If he didn't, he'd go mad.

In his *New York Times* bestselling book *A Whole New Mind: Why Right-Brainers Will Rule the Future,* author Daniel H. Pink writes about how, after nearly a century of the world being heavily

Awesomeness Tip
"The opposite of play isn't work. It's depression. To play is to act out and be willful, exultant, and committed as if one is assured of one's prospects."

dominated by left-brained people (engineers, lawyers, and software engineers, for instance), our world is moving toward an age of right-brained dominance. Essentially, creatively minded people will gain prominence and importance in the business world they never had before.

You're going to like this part: Pink has a whole chapter on the importance of play.

To Daniel H. Pink, play is more than just a break from the grind. It is an essential key to being successful. Besides giving us time to rest, playing actually improves our work by helping us think creatively and take in a larger picture outside of the focus of our work.

You've probably heard of the show *House,* on Fox. It's about a doctor, played by British actor/comedian Hugh Laurie, who's ridiculously brilliant at diagnosing diseases that other doctors miss, but he's also a pretty epic jerk. For a large percentage of each episode, House and his team of doctors are faced with a medical mystery. They try different treatments and narrow the possibilities down as each treatment fails, yielding a new symptom. At the forty-five-minute mark or so, they are usually stumped. Nothing is working.

And it's right around this point House ends up talking to Wilson, a doctor who is not on his team, but who is also House's only close friend. The conversation between House and Wilson is almost never about the actual case. It'll go something like this:

[Wilson says something about House's inability to form meaningful relationships.]

[House makes a snarky comment.]

Wilson: Your problem, House, is you don't realize you're really a great guy on the inside, waiting to get out, like the Grinch.

[Camera zooms in close on House's face as his eyes go wide.]

House: Guy on the inside . . . Grinch . . .

[House gets up abruptly and hobbles out of the room.]

[Later, in operating room, where House's team is preparing a do-or-die operation on the patient with the mystery illness. House barges into the room, usually pulling a cable out of a machine in the process.]

House: STOP!!! Stop the surgery! All this time, we were looking in the wrong place. The problem is inside the patient. He has grinchitis, a rare heart disorder where the patient's heart swells to three sizes too big.

[Patient is cured by a simple procedure.]

Sure, House is a fictional character, but that epiphany moment toward the end of each episode is an illustration of how House's playtime, when he goes and messes with Wilson, often draws out the brilliant solution he needs to do his job well.

Real life doesn't work out so neatly, of course, but the point is the same. When we take time out for the people and hobbies we love, we get better at doing our job and utilizing our talents.

// The rest of your life

Chick-fil-A is a hugely successful fast-food chain based in Georgia. They claim to have invented the chicken sandwich, which makes them a-okay in my book.

When asked about the best business decision he ever made, the company's founder, S. Truett Cathy, points to something you wouldn't expect: Choosing to keep every Chick-fil-A store closed on Sunday.

Think about that for a second: Chick-fil-A's chairman is saying his best business choice was to effectively eliminate 1/7th of his potential income.

S. Truett Cathy made that decision because he is a church-goer and firmly believes in a Sabbath. The Sabbath is a Jewish and Christian tradition which calls for one day out of every week to be spent away from work, either with loved ones or tinkering around the house, or reading a book, or watching football all day.

Whether you hold those beliefs or not, the act of taking a

step back from driving toward your goals can be wonderfully rejuvenating—a chance to recharge, relax, breathe, and spend time with the people in your life who really matter.

It's really important you give yourself an opportunity to relax now and then.

If you need an excuse, just say God told you to take a day off.

// Sometimes hobbies pay off

If you're not at the top of your game yet, if you're paying your dues on the way to dominating your world (see: Doing what you have to do so you can do what you want to do), you could argue taking the time to hone your talents is even more important.

My friend Jason, the writer, was saving up money to get married. Writing wasn't paying the bills, so Jason took a full-time job at a grocery store. The combination of being on his feet for eight hours performing tasks he didn't find at all interesting wore on him, but Jason still knew he had to work at his dream, so he spent at least an hour every day on writing projects and blog entries.

That little bit of time each day helped keep him on task. While he liked the people he worked with and served at the grocery store, he didn't want to spend the rest of his life ringing up artichokes. For about a year or so, writing was Jason's "hobby," at least until he could earn enough income to quit his job as a cashier.

I mentioned this in the chapter on school, but sometimes you just have to do what you have to do. What's important is keeping those goals in sight and working toward them even if they seem miles away from reality.

And even when your hobby isn't the same as your dream job, it'll pay off in one way or another. If you love cooking like Sonny does, it doesn't matter if it pays the bills, but I can guarantee it will get him a second date.

Part 4

HOW to DOMINATE TODAY, TOMORROW, and FOREVER

26

The Battle Never Ends

Congratulations! You've dominated your world!

Well, a few significant parts of it, anyway.

I mean, for today, at least.

I don't mean to be a downer, but becoming the hero of your world and kicking out the villains isn't just a BAM! POW! DONE kind of thing. Those villains will keep coming back.

That puppy is still sitting in that pet store window, and a new one will probably join it next week. Ninjas and vampires will never stop trying to control your time and money. Pirates will never stop trying to take advantage of you. I mean, they're villains—what did you expect? Peaceful surrender?

In his bestselling book *Outliers*, Malcolm Gladwell examined what it takes to be successful.

To do so, he studied the men and women who had *really*

dominated their world. He looked at Bill Gates, Michael Jordan, the Beatles, and professional hockey players from Canada.

He found that in order to reach that level of success, people needed three things:

1. To be in the right place at the right time for opportunities to present themselves.
2. To recognize and seize those opportunities when they appeared.
3. To work as hard as they could.

You'll notice that of those three things, only one is completely under your control: number 3, hard work.

But there's a trick with those things that are out of your control: An optimistic attitude and perseverance. You can't force a company to hire you or a record label to offer you a contract, but you can keep trying.

Perseverance is the cousin of hard work. It's one thing to begin a great project. Starting is easy. It's following through that's the killer.

When we start a project, no matter what it is, some inexplicable force in the universe steps up to stop us. You can call that force whatever you want, but there's no denying it's there. The stronger that force works against you, the more likely it is that your project is necessary, and the more important it is that you fight through to the end (see Chapter 6: Using ghosts as reverse guides).

This is why the world is littered with people who haven't dominated their world. They've all had dreams, but not all have had the guts to follow through and cross the finish line. Doing this takes an unbelievable amount of courage. You have no idea what's in store when you set out to accomplish a dream, just like Luke Skywalker had no idea what was ahead when he left the farm on Tatooine. What you *do* know is, the more you overcome, the greater a hero you will be.

// Success isn't always what you think

Finishing a goal doesn't mean you'll be rich and famous right away. (Besides, money will make you happy only if you give it away, remember?) You might fight the kind of adversity that few people have ever dreamed of and your project still might fail. At least in your terms.

But . . .

Falling short doesn't mean you've failed. Once you've followed through and finished what you started, it becomes easier next time, simply because you've done it before. Sometimes success is just accomplishing something that others rarely do.

It's like flying. When everything breaks down and you've plummeted to earth, you dust yourself off, look up at the sky, and say out loud, "Well, now I know what *doesn't* work."

> *Awesomeness Tip*
> "Practice makes improvement."
> —Josh Shipp

Then you take to the sky again.

27

The End Has a Start

Hopefully, this book has done a good job of explaining what the real world looks like for a teen like yourself. But just in case, I want to take a moment and review. If you've been nodding off while reading or holding the book in one hand and your Xbox controller in the other . . . wake up. Focus.

This is where it counts.

// Dominate YOUR world

By now, you should fully understand what it means to dominate your own world. After reviewing (and mocking) all of the cartoon villains, evildoers, and historical morons who tried to take over the world, we've determined it's a generally dumb idea that just doesn't really work. However, we have also discovered that there is one thing that's worth pursuing. By striving to dominate your world, you can overcome your villains, survive in any circumstance, and be the hero of your own epic story. In other words, your world can be dominated by one and only one person . . . YOU.

// Follow the Hero's Creed

We've discussed the two basic principles of the Hero's Creed. The first is that NO ONE else has the right to dominate your world. The second is that you don't have the right to dominate any one else's world. If you can stick with following these two rules, the rest of your life will be DRASTICALLY different. Will it be easy? No, not at all. Will it be worth it? Yes. I don't promise you much, but if take on the Hero's Creed seriously, your life and the way you view the world will definitely improve.

// Overcome your villains

I hope you can finally start to see the villains in your life for what they really are. Let's be honest: It's going to be tough, because we've learned that villains can be tricky. Sometimes they disguise themselves as your parents, your best friend, or even a simple commercial on TV. The villains are everywhere, and most people never even realize they are under attack. But now you do. It's your job to be the hero, overcome the villains, and—more important—help others in their quest as they come along behind you.

// How to dominate your days

Life is complicated. You have to balance relationships, school, work, hobbies, technology, driver's tests, etc. That's a whole lot of scenarios where you need to be on top of your game. Personally, I think being a teen today is a lot harder than when your parents were teens (don't tell them I said that; they'll get all defensive). You have so much going on and so many opportunities for success and failure. But remember, no matter what scenario you find yourself in, you can always remember the basic rules of the Hero's Creed. You can choose to look at all of your responsibilities as an overwhelming list that you'll never overcome, or as a string of day-by-day decisions that will add up over time. Remember, the best way to dominate all of your days is to take it one day and one challenge at a time.

// Everything changes . . . and everything stays the same

This is kind of a good news/bad news situation. In life, things will always be changing. By that I mean your circumstances will always be changing—including your friends, jobs, locations, living situations, roommates, etc. You'll date different people, you'll be hired and fired, you'll be let down, you'll let others down. Life is different every single day, and you will face a variety of challenges every time you crawl out of bed.

But then there's the good news. . . .

Everything stays the same! While you will always be facing these different challenges and having shoot-outs with villain after villain in all of these different circumstances, there are some things that never change.

The general principles such as the Hero's Creed never change. You will always and forever be the only person responsible for what happens with your life, in both the good and bad situations. In addition, the tactics used by the villains, while they seem to be shifting, will always be the same. They will focus on greed, pride, jealousy, and insecurity. When you learn to spot these villains, it will become easier and easier for you to get out of their way and handle them appropriately. The villains won't stop attacking you. In fact, if you're a real hero, they'll do everything they can to take you down. But this time you'll be ready for them.

// You must choose!

When you put down this book, you are going to make a decision, right?

Maybe you'll go to sleep or turn on the TV. Maybe you'll sit back and think through all of the crazy things I've thrown at you. Maybe you'll start to truly think about who you are or the friends that you hang out with. It could be that you'll start to research a new career or start studying for an upcoming test. You may even begin to analyze your life and start seeing individuals as the villains that they are.

Maybe you'll write a thank you letter/e-mail/text to a friend who, over time, has shown that he or she is a valuable ally.

Only you can make that decision.

Did you get that? I'll say it again. Only you can make that decision. As much as I'd love to waltz in and whip you into shape, I can't. From here on out, the decisions are up to you. But remember, the NEXT decision you make and every decision after that are steps that can take you in either a right or a wrong direction.

// Look around

Do you know what an audit is? It's an inspection. Your parents know what this word means. You might have heard the phrase "getting audited by the IRS." This means that the Internal Revenue Service, a government agency, is going to take the time to pore through every financial decision your parents made in the past year and determine if there has been any issues that need to be addressed. (If you ever want to freak out your parents sometime, answer the phone and say, "Hold on." Then look your dad in the eye and say, "It's the IRS. Something about an audit?" Pay attention to the look he gives you—that is the look of true fear!)

Hopefully, you haven't been audited by the IRS, but maybe it's time for you to take a personal life audit. You could chose to take a few minutes and review the identity section in Chapter 15. Get out a piece of paper and start answering those questions. If you're too lazy to browse back through the pages, here they are again:

1. What makes you unique?
2. What do you love? What do you hate?
3. What are you good at? What are you bad at?
4. What do you stand for? What do you stand against?

Now take some time and write down your identity statement—something that encompasses your life as your know it. It doesn't have to be too specific, but it should be something that kind of helps guide the decisions that you make every single day.

Next part of the audit: Write down a list of your five closest friends. Now these are tough questions, but I know you have the courage to answer them. Are your friends good people? Are they the heroes of their own stories or are they the villains taking over other people's lives . . . maybe even yours? If you were best friends with these five people for the rest of your life, would they make your life better or worse?

I know that this is difficult, but maybe you need to reconsider who you spend your time with. I know this could sting, like ripping off a bandage, but if you don't, you are allowing these zombies or these pirates to control you by demanding your attention.

Maybe you need to ask the same question about the person you are dating. Is he or she a pirate? A zombie? A puppy? You should really figure that out, because these decisions you're making with your boyfriend or girlfriend will impact your lives for a long, long time.

// The master plan

Once you've audited your life, it's time to make a list of goals.

Don't make your list just about how much money you want to make, or how many cars you want to have. Make goals that will tell a great story, a story worth retelling!

Making a million dollars isn't a great story. Making a million dollars, then providing clean water for one year for a million people in Africa, is.

More than generosity, though, make your goals about accomplishing what you want to accomplish. Dream big, and dream far in advance.

It's time to talk about what being a hero and dominating your world actually means. Nobody likes a hero who sits around watching YouTube all day long. Not. A. Hero. Heroes are awake! Heroes have passions! Heroes pursue epic goals to the ends of the earth and refuse to give up!

What are your goals? What could be changed, discovered, or invented all because of you? Who could be encouraged, rescued, or helped all because of you?

In five years, you might realize your goals have changed. Maybe you'll discover that being a doctor isn't for you. Maybe you'll want to be a musician instead. Maybe you'll feel called to something completely different. That's totally cool. Just make a new set of goals. That's part of a great story. A hero doesn't always accomplish what she set out to do. What she faces and learns along the way may give her a new mission. What's important is, she doesn't give up on pursuing who she is becoming. Ever.

Even if you *do* have your plans set out, you can't live five, or thirty, or even one year in the future. If you're going to drive across the country, you can't daydream about reaching the coast of Maine (or the coast of Oregon if you live on the East Coast, or either place if you live in the middle). Daydreaming is pointless; it doesn't get you anywhere.

First, you have to make sure your car can make the trip. Or that you even have a car. Or a driver's license, for that matter. Then you get in your car and start it up. Then you have to load up the tank and buy a map and some snacks for the road.

Then you just go. You face one mile at a time. That's all you can deal with right now.

You experience everything between you and your destination. You stick to the roads that keep you going in the right direction, even if you take the time to enjoy the scenic routes. Then, one day, you'll be there. You'll think about the sites you saw on your journey, and the people you met, and the friends you made, and that time in Nebraska when it was raining freakishly hard and your tire blew, and you didn't think you'd ever finish what you set out to do.

"I *did* make it," you'll think. "I've come all this way, and I'm here, and it feels awesome."

Then, here's what you do: You plan your next adventure and set off again.

It's your world, young champion, and you get to make your own master plan, but don't forget that there are a bunch of people out there who don't have this same luxury. Maybe one of your master plans can be to help them out along the way. In my opinion, a story worth retelling looks to help others that are outside of your relationships with your family, your friends, your school, and even your country.

// It IS a small world after all

If you are reading this book, I can safely assume two things about you:

1.   You can read. If you can't read, and you're somehow absorbing this information, then maybe you should submit yourself for government testing.
2.   You live in a place where this book is available, and therefore reside in one of the more prosperous countries in the world.

If those two things are true, you are one of the most fortunate people on the face of the planet. You already have more power, influence, and wealth than the vast majority of humanity.

Spider-Man's dearly departed Uncle Ben has a quote about this sort of thing: "With great power comes great responsibility." As a person with superpowers (and in the lens of the world, reading and living in a prosperous nation count as superpowers), you can choose to either use those powers selfishly and become a super villain or use them to protect and help others and become a superhero.

Remember, heroes are protectors and defenders, not just of themselves, but of those weaker than they. Heroes should be motivated by a sense of responsibility and a strong belief in justice to do more than simply sit back and bask in their glorious hero-ness.

Part of being a hero is being the world's greatest ally, even to people who you've never met and probably never will.

So, here is another audit question. Have you ever considered that the world isn't fair? Lucky for you and me, we were born in a time and place that allows us to do something about it. There is a mentality in the world today, even with a lot of teens, that says, "I want, I want, I want." But what would happen to your life if that became "I give, I give, I give"?

// Generosity is necessary

Being generous with what we have has many benefits, including feeling really great about yourself. But that's not why you should be generous. It's not about you.

It's about us, and how we're in it together. If we consistently use others and walk by our fellow man with our noses up and a closed hand, we hurt ourselves.

Call it what you want: Karma, the Golden Rule, whatever . . . wisdom means we see the world as a whole, look at it from a perspective other than our own. If we were broke and out of luck, we would need help. But if we rely only on the government, or on other, more generous people to do their part, we are only hurting ourselves. We are simply contributing to a broken system instead of doing something to try and fix it.

If you are dominating your own world, you have a gift, but it's not a gift that should be packed away deep inside you. It's a gift you need to share—teaching and helping others to choose to dominate their worlds.

For example, meet Zach Hunter.

Zach Hunter is an antislavery activist who launched Loose Change to Loosen Chains, a student-led effort to raise awareness and funds to end slavery all around the world. He's also written three books. When he realized there are actually 27 million slaves in the world today, he knew it wasn't enough just get all emotional about it. He took his emotions of outrage and disbelief and started a movement among his fellow students.

Oh, by the way, Zach was only twelve years old when he published his first book and is only nineteen years old right now! Now don't sit around and tell me that he had this and you don't. I'll tell you what he had: Passion. Zach determined at a young age that his life wasn't going to be about him and what he can accomplish. Zach determined at twelve years old that he was going to free slaves! Jeez! When I was twelve years old, I was probably in detention for being a jerk. What's the difference? I chose to mess around and see what I could get away with. Zach chose to use whatever talent he had to raise money in order to free slaves.

These are the decisions that we choose to make (or not make) every single day.

Or think about Bethany Hamilton. When she was thirteen, she was surfing off the coast of Hawaii and was attacked by a shark! In fact, she almost died because of how much blood she lost! Now if there is anyone who can complain about how unfair life is, it would be Bethany. But you know what? She overcame her ghosts, got back in the water, and taught herself to surf again . . . with only one arm! And not only did she learn, she went on to win fifth place at the National Surfing Championships in 2004, and took first place in the Open Women's division at the first stop on the Hawaii National Scholastic Surfing Association circuit.

I love the interview she gave on *Primetime Live* a few years back. She said, "I get tons of letters—stories of people that were going through a hard time and then they saw that I didn't give up on my dreams, I kept surfing—it helped them out a lot and that just shows that good can come out of like bad stuff like this." She is a true hero.

Talk about a situation of either getting bitter or better. She took an awful accident and is now using it to help teens overcome the villains in their lives.

These stories are everywhere. Some people choose to let the villains (and sharks) dominate their lives, while others—heroes like Zach and Bethany—stand up and fight back to overcome these villains. So, who will you be?

Now is the time to decide! Are you going to choose the hard thing because it's the right thing? Drop that bad friend? Make that pirate walk the plank? Develop your own programming so you can finally get all those robots off your back? Say NO to the ninjas and tell them to go trick someone else? Quit following those vampires and learn that all they want is to strip you of your identity?

Are you going to do it?

You are you. You are the hero of your own world and it is waiting to be dominated by you. Remember, if you don't do it, there is a long list of villains who are ready and waiting to take over.

No more excuses. Like I said, there are no secrets that will automatically fix everything, but a series of decisions to make to live a life worth remembering. And this is one of those moments.

This is a moment that can change your life forever.

This is a moment that, one day, you can look back on and declare that everything changed the moment I shut that book. Or, you can put this book on your shelf and forget about it. It can collect cobwebs and mold, and someday you can put it in a garage sale because you need some extra cash to pay off your growing credit-card debt.

Let this book be your guide. Come back to it often to remind yourself of what it looks like to dominate your own world. Keep editing your ID statement so you will always know who you are and how you relate to the world around you. Come back often to get a refresher course on the villains in your life and make sure you remember how to keep them far, far away.

// The best world domination stories live on forever

One of the things about movies and books is that they end. The hero gets the girl, or defeats the bad guy, or becomes a better person. In a movie, it takes a couple hours. In a book, a little longer. But generally speaking, every story that we watch, read, tell, or listen to will end.

I think this is why we love simple stories but life can sometimes seem a little difficult. Why? Our real life doesn't have that finality. Once we overcome a great obstacle, something else takes its place. Once you've fought through and earned your college degree, you face the new story of finding a career you love. Once you find your career path, you enter into the story of finding a partner to spend your life with. Once you find a partner to spend your life with, maybe you will enter the story of parenthood, and you become a part of your child's story, which will continue on.

This is going to sound discouraging at first, but the quest to dominate your story won't end until, well, you do. But the great thing about dominating your world is that every decision that was made along your story was a decision that you made to become more and more of who you truly are at your core. This will make you happy. And while I still have a lot to learn, just like you, one thing I've learned is that if you can be happy, you can pretty much handle anything that comes your way.

So, now I leave you with a simple scenario. You will always face conflict, the villains will never stop their attacks, and there will always be obstacles as you seek to fulfill your world domination plan.

And you have two choices:

1. You can face those obstacles and those villains head-on, because it will continually make you a better person. It will

shape you into a remarkable storyteller with life experiences that made the world a better place. You will live like a hero and die a hero's death.

Or . . .

2.   You can give up. You can run and hide. You can numb the conflicts of life with drugs and alcohol and sex and greed, right up until the day you die. Your story will suck.

But here's something I've learned: The best stories don't end with you. The best stories live on through your friends and family, and the lives you've had an impact on. That's the thing about living a great life: It's infectious.

If you want to infect the world with hope, protect those who can't protect themselves. If you want to live a life based on truth and not on the false advertisements and greed of others, then there is only one thing left for you to do:

Choose.

Choose to overcome your villains.

Choose to dominate your world.

You know how to do it.

Now go.

In your face, but on your side,

// josh

ACKNOWLEDGMENTS

Dear Reader,

The following is a list of smart/attractive/wonderful/caring/supportive people who you probably don't know, along with a lot of inside jokes you probably won't get. Just deal with it. No one is making you read this.

To all the people on this list, you have each made my life incredible, and I owe each of you a kidney. Sadly, I only have two. Cage match!

Sarah Shipp: I love you.

London Shipp: This is gonna be fun.

Rodney and Christine Weidenmaier: You are two truly incredible humans.

Alex and Roxanne Petruncola: I'm honored to be a part of your family.

Gary Jones: Thanks for teaching me how to live life.

Jane Sodowsky: Others saw punk kid; you saw potential.

Lettie Dilbeck: DECA was the car. Thanks for loaning me the keys.

Kathy McRice: You mean so much to me.

Tom Colley: Teaching and entertaining go hand in hand.

Patsy Sellars: You saw my success way before I did.

Jon Fortt: Your wisdom floors me.

David Tieche: Write your dang book!

Josh Keller: Boston Marathon, baby!

Russell Pierce: Your phone messages make me weep with joy.

Jeremy Hern: My guns are bigger than yours. The end.

Jason Jones: I miss you.

Ben VanMeter: Excellent choice, sire!

Jeff Revenaugh: Thanks for all the rides.

Jeff Wootton: Heeeeyap!

Sam Glenn: Thanks for all your early guidance.

Chris Fisher: The best wingman ever.

Ezra Gordon: So excited for your future! I know him!

Kindle Smyth: What would Mike Mammoth do?

Erin Niumata: You are responsible for this being on the shelf.

David Wenzel: Brother?

Michael Colletto: I don't know how you do it. Have you hacked my
    brain?

Jordan Green: Great work, Jordan! You sure you're a 7?

Molly Young: Without you this would be nothing but *Star Wars*
    references.

Brett VanTil: The man of mystery who holds it all together.

Corey Petrick: You started all this, hipster.

Santino Stoner: All of our conversation make me wanna change
    the world.

Kirk Flatow: The big brother I never had. Shake and Bake.

Julie Biagini: Navel to spine!

Carol Siebenmorgen: Good evening, Carol.

Eric Diaz: Don't be mad you're this far down on the list.

Else Sinsisigalli: My fellow Kenyan/hippie.

Steve McGowan: Me. You. Ocean. Soon.

John Heinlein and Mel Bjorn: No more board games with you guys.

Barb Acosta: Love you, mom!

Tim Schenone: Thanks, coach!

Donald Miller: Thanks for leading the way.

Gabe Lyons: I'm flattered to be a part of what you've built.

Bob Goff: You've changed my perspective. Forever.

Ken and Aimee VanMeter: You set the bar so high. In marriage and in salsa.

Alyse Diamond: You just plain get it. Thank you!

Lisa Senz and the St. Martin's Team: Thrilled to be a part of this family.

Jamie Oliver: I still owe you lunch.

Frank Kern: You are the sensai.

Tony Hawk: Thanks for the kind words.

Craig Mitchell: Thanks, roomie.

The Roth Family: Rick and Baby Mama!

Bobby Gruenwald: This is better than a tweet, yes?

Brian Fernandes: Judd Apatow who?

And a Goat: Dot Com.

ABOUT JOSH SHIPP

Josh Shipp is a teen advice guru, motivational speaker, marathon runner, and undisputed guitar hero. With more than a decade of hands-on, real-world experience, Josh has earned an international reputation as a leading authority on teen communication that's "in your face, but on your side." Abandoned and abused as a child, and raised in a dozen different foster homes, Josh has taken his past of hurt and neglect, turned it around, and used it as a catalyst for helping others.

Seen on MTV, CNN, NBC, FOX, Comedy Central, and featured in the *Los Angeles Times* and *Inc. Magazine*'s "30 Under 30: America's Coolest Young Entrepreneurs," Josh's inspiring personal story and life-changing message has reached more than a million teens . . . and counting. Say "hi" at HeyJosh.com.

Founded in 2008, Hey Josh LLC is an integrated media platform that uses Josh Shipp's unique life experience and communication style to deliver meaningful video, Web, and published experiences for teens and young adults, and those who influence them positively.